Quarterly Essay

Quarterly Essay is published four times a year by Black Inc., an imprint of Schwartz Media Pty Ltd. Publisher: Morry Schwartz.

ISBN 978-1-86395-701-4 ISSN 1832-0953

Subscriptions – 1 year (4 issues): $59 within Australia incl. GST. Outside Australia $89.
2 years (8 issues): $105 within Australia incl. GST. Outside Australia $165.

Payment may be made by Mastercard or Visa, or by cheque made out to Schwartz Media. Payment includes postage and handling.

To subscribe, fill out and post the subscription card or form inside this issue, or subscribe online:

www.quarterlyessay.com
subscribe@blackincbooks.com
Phone: 61 3 9486 0288

Correspondence should be addressed to:

The Editor, Quarterly Essay
37–39 Langridge Street
Collingwood VIC 3066 Australia
Phone: 61 3 9486 0288 / Fax: 61 3 9486 0244
Email: quarterlyessay@blackincbooks.com

Editor: Chris Feik. Management: Sophy Williams, Caitlin Yates. Publicity: Anna Lensky. Design: Guy Mirabella. Assistant Editor: Kirstie Innes-Will. Production Coordinator: Siân Scott-Clash.

CLIVOSAURUS | The Politics of
Clive Palmer

Guy Rundle

Saturday, 3 July 2014, and outside Coolum, along David Low Way on the Sunshine Coast of Queensland, the cars were backed up for a stretch, heading into the Palmer Coolum Resort. It was the weekend before the new Senate would begin sitting, and the gates of the combination golf resort, gated community and dinosaur park had been thrown open by its owner, Clive Palmer, alleged billionaire and newly elected MP for Fairfax. Weeks earlier, every household in the electorate of Fairfax had received, Wonka-style, a Palmer-yellow pamphlet/invitation to the venue, which normally charged a cool hundred bucks per family for entry. It must have been particularly appreciated by those who had been – as reported in the *Australian* – recently laid off by the resort, as business nosedived. Still, there was free access to the dinosaurs, and an Elvis concert, and, as the brochure advertised, a series of rolling seminars by Palmer United Party (PUP) luminaries, with buffet ...

Palmer had purchased the former Hyatt Regency Coolum in 2011, at a time when its chief attraction – and a major source of revenue for the nearby town of Coolum – was hosting the Australian PGA Championship.

When Palmer took ownership and announced plans to turn it into a theme park featuring more than a hundred animatronic dinosaurs, the PGA warned him that too many distractions visible from the course would endanger the accreditation. They had in mind something like a plastic T-Rex looming over the first tee. Subsequent pictures of the resort showed a plastic T-Rex looming over the first tee. The PGA accreditation was duly rescinded, depriving Coolum of huge revenues, not recouped by the animatronic additions, in honour of which Clive had wanted to rename the place "Jurassic Park." Amazingly, there were intellectual property issues, so "Jurassic Park" became "Palmersaurus."

On the first day of free entry, not only were cars stretching back, but people were hiking on foot (Joe Hockey's poor people, presumably). There was a festive air, a touch of Woodstock. Inside the long buffet tent beside the Coolum Rooms conference centre, food was being ladled out, and one tried not to think of Jonestown. The conference centre was in one direction from the park's main crossroads with its proud welcoming sign (Asian food this way!), the dinosaur trail stretched the other – dozens of the things, brown, plastic, leathered and, as we now know, probably inaccurate (dinosaurs were most likely semi-feathered). The kids dragged their parents to the trail, but, well, after a while, all dinosaurs are alike. By coronosaurus they were lagging, by iguanadon they wanted to go the other way – by which point the parents had become bloody-minded. "I donnnnn't wannnnn't to see any more dinosaurs," said a small girl. "We're seeing the dinosaurs," said her dad, pulling her along. The weekend was rich in analogy.

Over at the Coolum Rooms, other big beasts were gathering. The PUP's Queensland senator, Glenn Lazarus, the "brick with eyes," rolled in with a posse of good ol' boys, enormous men in male bling, tapping on BlackBerries as they walked. Palmer's other media guy, Andrew Crook – improbably but inevitably trading as Crook Media – buzzed around, harassed and bothered. Then a golf cart pulled up, and Crook imposed himself in front of the two camera crews as His Cliveness struggled out. It took about three moves, and images of religious cults yielded to *Caddyshack*.

The "seminars" were rolling short speeches and Q&As, with Clive speaking three times a day over both days, and Lazarus, Queensland MP Alex Douglas and West Australian senator Zhenya "Dio" Wang making up the undercard. Jacqui Lambie was around but not speaking; so was Queensland Liberal National Party (LNP) defector Carl Judge, who had the demeanour of a hostage being treated well. Folks drifted in and out, in their tens and twenties for the minor players, but surging to fill the 400-seat hall – really, like an enormous garage converted to a spare room – when Clive appeared. Milling outside, most were happy to say they hadn't voted for him, had come for the dinosaurs, the vintage cars (in a vast humidicrib building), but were interested in what he had to say. It was a Sunshine Coast mix: tradies and their families, sea-changers with not that much to do, a few people from old Coast families, and the long-ago hippies and alternative types you get on such coasts, in folksy '70s gear and with the occasional mandala tattoo.

On stage, Clive had a routine for them. He spoke of youthful dreams and hopes for a better Australia, of the inspiration of John F. Kennedy, and of his belief in the power of love. He told of going into politics because the Campbell Newman government, which he had supported into power, had turned against ordinary Queenslanders so badly that he felt he had to do something. "I went home and said to my wife, 'Jeez, things are so bad I might have to run for the Senate,' and she said, 'Well, don't do that, you might win – run for the House instead' – so here I am." That got a mild laugh, and then he told a story we would hear many times, about four old ladies who pooled what was left of their pension cheques every fortnight and took a trip to the cinema – "and if the Medicare co-payment was imposed, they wouldn't be able to do that anymore." There was no budget emergency, he said, Australia had the third-lowest public debt in the OECD. What we needed was to build the country. And we would do it, with love.

It's fair to say that the crowd was not fired up with enthusiasm, and it showed in the questions. Many of those who had voted for Clive, and even more of those who hadn't, were concerned about the deficit, which they assessed in the way they had been encouraged to by the major parties – as a family budget, in the "can't spend what you don't have" manner. The price of money and Keynesian demand weren't what they wanted to hear about. There was also disquiet at Palmer's plan to deal with boat-borne refugees by running cheap flights from Jakarta for all comers. If this was populism, it was a strange way to do it.

The energy crackled again when Glenn Lazarus got up and began to talk about his family, his footy and how his mum had propelled him into his greatest achievements. There was a pause. "Any questions?" said the MC. Someone asked something about the budget. Lazarus stumbled, "Well, uh, gosh, let me ..." "Before you answer that, Glenn," the MC piped up, "maybe you could tell us about some of the experiences on the field that might help you in parliament?" Lazarus's enormous form relaxed and he leaned in. "Oh, we've had some torrid tussles ..." he went on, and the crowd relaxed too.

Then Clive leapt into the cart, and we all followed him to fields beside the food court, where the king of the Gold Coast Elvis impersonators, Dean Vegas – thin '50s black-leathers Elvis, not white-jumpsuit-thrombosis Elvis – gave us all the hits, and announced in character, "Y'know I ain' never ha' much time for politics, but I took one look at Clive and I knew this was someone I could support." An endorsement from Elvis! (Mr Vegas has run for mayor of the Gold Coast at least three times.)

Seated before the stage on a rise, surrounded by family and retinue, Clive looked pleased. There was a vaguely Roman imperial air, and a suggestion that Mr Vegas would survive the cull, unlike the half-time act, a grinning X Factor contestant in spangles and follow-me-home-and-swap-preferences-with-me boots, who unwowed the crowd. Later that night, Clive stood up with the scratch band in the open-air food court and belted out "The Purple People Eater," a party piece he's been doing since he was a kid on the Gold Coast in the 1960s. Everyone had a good time, munching on okay food, listening to the hits and memories.

Even then, an early point in my encounters with Palmer, I didn't know what to think. On the one hand, we had just had two full days in which anyone could rock up and ask questions of their new MP and one of their state's senators, and get some straightforward answers. As politics, it was more open and direct than most major party MPs would take a chance on. But it couldn't be ignored that it was taking place on palatial grounds owned by the MP himself, and there was more than a touch of *Dallas* about it. Throughout the rolling speeches, I didn't have the sense Palmer was telling people what they wanted to hear. Quite the contrary: on refugees, the deficit and some of the budget measures – penalising the young unemployed, for example – he appeared noticeably to the left of many in the assembled crowd. Discussions in the foyer after each speech (I sat through the thoughts of Clive four times in two days) seemed to bear this out. "I still think it matters how much money we owe," one sixty-something Palmer voter, in rural Sunday best, told me, his wife nodding by his side. Others were of the same opinion, wanting to tie the deficit to immigration, and impatient with Palmer's fly-'em-in idea. "Whatever happens, we've got to stop the boats." Why had the speaker, a Maroochydore sea-changer, not voted down-the-ticket Coalition? "Oh, Somlyay [the former Liberal MP for Fairfax]? We called him the periscope – he only came up once every three years," she laughed. "I thought I'd give Clive a go."

"I thought I'd give him a go" was what you heard a lot from this crowd, and it seemed a funny sort of populist movement – something the PUP had been labelled from the start – that didn't consolidate fluke success by telling the public exactly what it wanted to hear. But then, a glance at the figures suggested it wasn't much of a populist movement at all, with Palmer scraping in in Fairfax with 26 per cent of the primary vote, no other PUP lower-house figure coming close, and only Lazarus among the Senate lists gaining a respectable primary vote. The Palmer phenomenon appeared to be driven by other forces: the man's heart-on-sleeve passions, imagined or real, and the tumbling mathematics of a broken electoral system. Who was Clive really, and what did his great political success mean, really? It seemed important to find out. But the next day there was no time. The *Australian* called the party over, with Hedley Thomas revealing that the money for the PUP campaign had come from funds earmarked as payment by the Chinese company CITIC to Palmer's Mineralogy company for port services. The op-ed pages, then and for days after, were filled with denunciations. Palmer, for his part, made it clear that the budget would be torn to shreds. A strange and portentous period in our political history had begun.

The courtyard of the Senate in Parliament House, with its tasteful grey stepping stones and its carefully placed trees – singly here and there, best when burst into autumn flame – was designed, no doubt, with an idea of dignity and quiet repose. But that has rarely been the use to which it has been put these past twenty-five years, becoming instead a staging point for press conferences, angled to take advantage of the leafy background, allowing pollies to give the impression that they are anywhere else than in Canberra. At any given time, there are usually a few news crews setting up their equipment for the next, or packing up after the last, giving the space the weird appearance of a nature park to observe media politics in its (un)natural habitat. Most prominent MPs do a presser here every now and then.

From the moment Clive Frederick Palmer arrived in Canberra, it was as though he had barely been out of it. More mornings than not, or so it seemed, an announcement would hit inboxes, often no more than half an hour before time, and the members of the press gallery would wearily grab their styrofoam cups of cold coffee and race down to hear what Clive had to say now. August 28 was no exception. Clive was there when we got down: expansive, enormous in his trademark blue pinstripe suit, any sense of menace that customarily attaches to tycoons somewhat undermined by his rougeish apple-cheeks and the '70s pageboy haircut he has remained faithful to over the decades.

Beside him was South Australia's Labor premier Jay Weatherill, painfully thin beside all this Clive. They were here so Clive could take another whack at Joe Hockey's budget, and in particular its measure to charge a seven-dollar payment for Medicare bulk-billed visits. By now that was an old story, and the only good angle on it was whether Clive would stick to his commitment that there would be "no co-pay ever," given recent deals Palmer and his party had made with the government on other matters. The *Australian* was also pursuing how Palmer's successful push into parliament had been funded. But as this line of inquiry got underway, another question was fired across the bows: "Is there any truth to the report that you walked out on Question Time on Monday to keep watch over your Palmer United Party senators?" We then got what was, by the measure of any media age, far too much information.

"Well, I first of all left parliament on Monday to go to the toilet, and that was the reason I got up and left: it was a pressing act of nature," said Clive, as radio journos tried to hold still their on-camera mikes while squirming, "and having done that act most successfully, and feeling much relieved" – he paused – "I decided I'd take a brisk walk because I was feeling much lighter," and at that moment it's fair to say that someone could have waved documents proving that Clive had the Beaumont children in a cellar somewhere and it would have failed to register. Everyone was dealing with the image of Clive, enormous man-baby, seated, swaddled on the throne, sending a Clive-class sub into the open water. Weatherill gave the impression of trying to drill into the earth, and Clive took a few more questions, and then, having made his, erm, drop, and avoided full scrutiny by the media pack, signed off once more.

"Feeding the chooks," his sometime mentor Joh Bjelke-Petersen called it, and in this encounter Clive had added an extra twist, a measure of his dislike of relentless press scrutiny on matters he didn't wish to speak about. He was feeding us shit and we were eating it up, because we needed the colour, and Clive had given us more over the past months than the rest of the parliament combined – from his toilet habits, to his assertion on Q&A that the Chinese were "mongrels" who "shoot their own people," to his habit of storming out of interviews.

But of course the real purpose of the presser had been achieved: to announce, Chevy Chase-style, that the Medicare co-payment was still dead, as were a range of other measures that Hockey and Abbott were trying to throw at the Australian public, wrapped up in the budget.

In previous appearances, either in this hallowed courtyard or during one of his barnstorming pressers through the corridors of the Senate offices, Palmer had triumphantly announced the results of his negotiations on the mining and carbon taxes, both of which he had pledged to abolish in the 2013 election campaign, but whose repeal he had blocked so as to preserve welfare, tax and super measures attached to them. In other words, he and the PUP had done a deal with the elected government in the lower house, allowing it to pass legislation it had campaigned on, while to a degree rejecting measures it hadn't announced.

Each such announcement had been treated as some sort of brain-snap sell-out by a mercurial lunatic. Yet by now Palmer had often declared his commitment to rejecting the most Brutopian features of the budget: he clearly saw them as being in a different class to other measures. As he remarked, the budget was "heartless and cruel" and "will cause many Australians undue pain, all based on a fairy tale they have concocted that Australia is in some kind of debt crisis." It was "a breach of promises made to the people of Australia by Prime Minister Tony Abbott and a betrayal of the trust the Australian people have put in government."

By the time he had come to make the potty remarks in the courtyard, it was clear to most that the Abbott government had started to back away from the budget. The government was now looking for something on which to refocus the nation's attention, and was soon rewarded with the advance of ISIS in Iraq. Palmer and the PUP had pretty much seen off a series of measures that would have made crucial changes to what remains of the social-democratic Australian state. Yet the press gallery was still waiting for the "next sell-out," and what was implied in Palmer's stand – a moral seriousness, out of whatever motives – was being ignored.

*

Handed down on 13 May 2014, the budget had sent a shockwave through the nation, with its proposed cuts and extra charges that the Coalition had not only not mentioned in the election campaign, but had also explicitly ruled out. The planned seven-dollar co-payment for all Medicare bulk-billed visits was the first attack on the universality of the service since it had become bipartisan policy in the late 1980s. In education, the government said it would bring in higher university fees and impose real interest rates on student loans. A complex and seemingly capricious scheme for unemployment benefits had been announced, in which the young jobless would come on and off the dole for six months at a time while they searched for work.

The public reacted with widespread anger and dismay to the budget, and many voicing such feelings had voted for Abbott – indeed, many had switched from Gillard/Rudd to Abbott partly on the grounds that the Labor government had run up a worrying amount of public debt. Had they been paying closer attention, they would have noticed that Team Abbott's campaign promises were flatly contradictory: no new taxes, retention of several Labor programs (particularly the Gonski education plan and the NDIS), and yet at the same time the "budget emergency" would be swiftly paid down. The Liberal Party knew that the public's impatience with Labor, stoked by a relentlessly propagandistic Murdoch press, did not extend to many of its social policies or the sort of Australia it had created – one in which a degree of social democracy and economic nationalism remained, even as sections of the economy and culture were transformed by neoliberal measures. Underestimating this attachment had killed the Howard government in 2007, and Abbott wasn't about to let it kill his chance in 2013. Had he been possessed of more courage, he would have gone to the public seeking a mandate for change, with no strings attached, and accepted a lower majority in exchange for it. Instead he promised everything, adding commitments as he went – no cuts to the ABC, no changes to super arrangements – until it was clear, by virtue of its contradictions, that the party's platform was a duplicitous one.

Something would have to give, and the budget was where it started. The near-immediate public rejection was fuelled by the plain oddness of some of the measures, which bore the marks of too-clever-by-half Treasury suggestions that had not been weeded out by a sensible politician: why impose a payment for medical services on low-income people, proclaim that all such measures were part of a common sacrifice – and then divert the proceeds into a nebulous research fund? Why combine tertiary-fee hikes with a rise in student-loan interest rates, so that the fees for a professional course suddenly loomed decades into someone's future? Why take the impatience many Australians felt with welfare dependency and turn it into sympathy for "dole bludgers" by imposing a system that made life planning impossible? From the moment the budget hit, commentators began puzzling over it, less in the manner of economic analysts, more in the spirit of CSI professionals assessing a pile-up of bodies on a desert road, looking for clues as to what went so horribly wrong that there could be so much blood everywhere. The Coalition's supporters were dismayed, its opponents jubilant, and everyone else was a little stunned.

But Clive Palmer wasn't, or if he was, he wasn't for long. About as soon as the budget hit the table, he was railing against it. To the attentive politics-watchers, this came as no surprise. Back in January 2014, he had come out against the National Commission of Audit, the body established to identify possible cuts: "Abbott's audit team are unqualified muppets ... These people aren't interested in outcomes for Australians." But at that stage his public image was still that of a Queensland coal baron who had once been Joh Bjelke-Petersen's spinmeister, and his remarks – about the budget emergency and debt crisis being vastly exaggerated, if not confected – were little heard.

On 14 May, though, when he announced that he wouldn't be backing the key welfare savings measures, people began to sit up and take notice. If Labor and the Greens stonewalled as expected, without Palmer's three Senate PUPs nothing would go through. Yet it was assumed by most that this stance was a stack of bargaining chips, which Clive would throw into the pot as required. Through May and June, the Abbott government was preoccupied with trying to sell the budget, first to rattled pundits in the right-wing commentariat, then to the public at large. The Coalition strate-gists knew Palmer had scores to settle with the Queensland LNP, and interests to pursue, but on welfare spending they assumed he'd come round in the end. Besieged on all fronts, they put off Senate negotiations until June. Late June. They were already hoping that the bloc agreement between the PUP and the Australian Motoring Enthusiast Party member, Ricky Muir, would fall apart, and that one of Palmer's senators – Jacqui Lambie from Tasmania, a feisty ex-soldier, single mum on benefits and former candidate for Liberal pre-selection – would peel off almost immediately and sit as an independent. That would give them six independent crossbenchers with whom to stitch up a deal, thus cutting Palmer out entirely. There was reason to wait and see how it all shook out.

Besides, Clive was being assailed on his other fleshy flank, with a relentless campaign against him run out of the *Australian*. In 2013, the national broadsheet had started taking a serious interest in Clive. Had it ever been tempted to turn to other matters, Clive had solved that by announcing in September that Wendi Deng Murdoch was a Chinese spy who had been assigned to marry and monitor Rupert on behalf of her Beijing masters. From that point on, the paper practically had a full-time Clive correspondent, and throughout the first half of 2014 they kept up a relentless stream of investigation into and commentary on Palmer's business dealings, personal behaviour and peccadilloes. Hedley Thomas was burrowing into the relationship between Palmer's Mineralogy and CITIC. As the inauguration of the new Senate neared, the *Australian* established that Palmer was at war with his Chinese partner: CITIC accused him of overcharging for their proposed massive Pilbara development. By June, Thomas was on the verge of publishing his more sensational revelations about campaign funding, while the remainder of the paper kept up a stream of less-relevant and niggling attacks – from allegations that Palmer had plagiarised part of a speech from John F. Kennedy, to scuttlebutt about his personal jets, to reports of fits of rage at Coolum. Palmer was an MP and a party leader, and a rich man, and could not reasonably object – though object he did – to the coverage. But it could also not be ignored that the *Australian* was paying a lot more attention to Clive's doings than to those of other politically engaged, very rich men, such as James Packer, Frank Lowy and, for that matter, Rupert Murdoch.

By mid-June, with the Senate session bearing down, the public and media perception of Palmer remained fixed. He was a populist out of Queensland, with no electoral base to speak of, an offbeat schtick and a willingness to take whatever position would jam up the government. At the moment he was taking a noticeably "left" line (though no one used that term) on social welfare, but that would shift. One thing that wasn't going to change was his relentless anti-environmentalism. With Clive having proposed not only that the carbon tax be abolished but also that businesses be reimbursed, and with a billion-dollar gamble on the Galilee Basin in play, that was a given. He had already informed the public the Greens were in league with the CIA, presumably in some back-channel war with Wendi Deng and the Chinese Communist Party. If there was one thing the increasingly beleaguered Coalition could rely on, it was that there wouldn't be any surprises there. Until, of course, he appeared at a press conference in the Great Hall of Parliament House, on 25 June, side by side with Al Gore.

*

Weeks later, a veteran of green politics, reflecting on that scene – the portly Palmer beside the thickened-out Gore, the former talking of his conversion to the science of anthropogenic global warming, the latter welcoming a mendicant to the fold – laughed ruefully and said, "I still can't quite believe it. But now, now it seems just the sort of thing Clive would always have done."

The general public concurred – with the first part. The presser – at which Palmer announced that although he would still be voting to repeal the carbon tax, he and his party would be voting to retain the Clean Energy Finance Corporation and the Renewable Energy Target scheme – was a stunning development, throwing assumptions about the political alignment of the new Senate into further doubt. For the Abbott government this was a nightmare: it had been relying on the carbon-tax repeal to go straight through on 7 July, the first day of sitting, and provide a much-needed visible and dashing victory. Now it was going to be held up, as the PUPs were either cajoled and bullied into passing the whole bill, or the renewables measures were disentangled from it. The clean victory would be as dirty as the industry the Coalition parties were trying to serve.

The meeting of Palmer and Gore, and the agreement for a green hero to give his imprimatur to a coal baron while saving the Australian renewables sector and targets, had been put together by three Greens veterans, now out of front-line parliamentary politics: Richard Denniss and Ben Oquist of the Australia Institute, both former chiefs-of-staff to Christine Milne (and Oquist to Bob Brown as well), and Don Henry, the recently departed head of the Australian Conservation Foundation. Oquist and Denniss were both firmly oriented towards getting concrete results, and both inside and outside the Greens they had been increasingly critical of stalwart or oppositional politics. Henry was connected to Gore through his ACF role. Oquist had been involved, for the Greens, in preference negotiations with Palmer, especially around the Queensland Senate, where each party needed the other for a quota but would have great difficulty explaining the swap to its voters. Palmer later claimed that he had had another line to Gore through the John F. Kennedy Library Foundation, but it is just faintly possible that this was a convenient non-truth.

For the Abbott government, the first year was beginning to acquire a shape – and that shape was as a cummerbund, worn round the ample belly of the PUP's irrepressible leader, Sydney Greenstreet minus the fez. The *coup de fou* with Al Gore was followed by the festival of democracy at Coolum, and in the next week the Senate of the forty-fourth parliament of the Commonwealth of Australia convened for its first session.

*

The web page on which the upper house posts its order of business is titled "Dynamic Red," a popular shade of paint. Perhaps it is their little joke, because the Senate most often give the appearance of a reading of the minutes at a tennis club. But on 7 July it was all go, right from seven in the morning, when the new senators were doorstopped at the entrance for their first thoughts. Beneath a grey drizzly sky that matched his otherworldly complexion, the libertarian David Leyonhjelm spoke for many, if not all, of them when asked how he felt: "Terrified, but I'm sure we'll get through."

With no more than a day's induction, and with representatives of all parties wandering around trying to find their offices in the featureless and symmetrical building, the new senators were expected to consider a cascade of legislation: carbon-tax repeal, mining-tax repeal, repeal of Labor's Future of Financial Advice reforms, and passage of the privatisation-prompting Asset Recycling Initiative, just for a start.

When the chamber convened, there was a brief flurry as the Greens nominated Senator Scott Ludlam for president, a role that usually goes without challenge to the government party. So it did now, but the vote gave occasion for a general shake-hands-and-good-to-know-you meet-and-greet, with Senator Eric Abetz, Coalition leader in the upper house, being about as relaxed as an Austrian-Tasmanian adenoidal god-botherer can manage. He had been a bit less friendly in private in the hurried negotiations in the week or so before the Senate met, some crossbench staff said, but when asked about the new senators he had remarked, "Well, they're all God's children."

The good feeling didn't last long – only until the PUPs and other crossbenchers joined with the Labor–Green bloc to block the carbon-tax repeal, on the grounds that the anti-renewables measures had not yet been stripped out of it. With Clive sitting in the visitors benches and watching benignly over his yellow-and-black clad senators – the big banana watching over the cuttings – the PUPs did what Palmer had said for weeks they would, and ruined the Abbott government's potential first triumph.

Despite all that had gone before, the Coalition senators appeared shocked and surprised. They scurried over to the crossbenchers, all cordiality gone, and berated them with hand gestures and clutched foreheads. From where I sat in the gallery, it was like watching a big family argument through the front window of a restaurant. The Coalition did not do itself any favours: crossbenchers would later say that Abetz and his minions were rude and patronising, telling the PUPs that they didn't understand what they were doing, had the wrong end of the stick, and so on. The treatment hardened the PUPs' resolve, and gave them a very succinct lesson in how they were viewed by the Coalition establishment. They were always going to pass the repeal, when a deal could be done, but Abetz's inept handling of the situation contributed to days of delay, and fuelled the growing impression that the Abbott government had even less control of the political process than the benighted Rudd–Gillard–Rudd outfit.

The next day, Ricky Muir spoke in favour of the Australian Renewable Energy Agency, which Palmer had pledged to support because it was making a profit, employing many people, and, "If you're going to get rid of it, at least sell it off for a couple of billion." The sight of Muir, an unassuming former sawmiller (and shop steward and manager) tagged with a bogan revhead image because of his party and a YouTube video of him mucking around with kangaroo droppings, defending the funding of wind farms and solar panels drove everyone on Team Abbott a little mad. They had counted on the PUP–Muir bloc being to the right of the Coalition – and, together with Leyonhjelm and the Family First senator, Bob Day, being the six crossbenchers they needed to pass legislation. Now it became clear that Palmer meant what he said: every bill would have to be fought for, line by line, amendment by amendment. The fortnight ended with the stalling of not only the carbon-tax repeal, but also the mining-tax repeal and the assets-recycling program – here the PUPs supported a Ludlam-led Greens move to rename it the "Encouraging Privatisation Bill." At the end of the first week of the new Senate, Tony Abbott had started to take a renewed interest in the search for Malaysia Airlines Flight MH370, and then came the shooting down of MH17.

*

By now, Clive Palmer and the PUPs were gaining a visibility they had previously lacked, despite the relentless media coverage. "I like him," more than one inner-city leftie told me, half-whispering. Few people outside Queensland had followed the ins and outs of Palmer's feud with Campbell Newman and its role in propelling him into front-line politics, and they had assumed his domestic politics would be right-wing market fundamentalism, red in tooth and claw. Taking a position against the "emergency" budget had drawn some attention, but most still assumed it was a temporary manoeuvre. With the Gore appearance, and then with the stonewalling of the carbon tax, it was clear that Palmer meant business, and that he was landing blows on the government at a time when opposition leader Bill Shorten appeared to be fatally lacking in energy and will. Palmer also had something of the wry impishness that Bob Brown had brought to the leadership of the Greens, and that Christine Milne, for all her virtues, could not project. It was a sense of being in control, setting the agenda and making the government bend the knee.

It had been accompanied by a fair bit of lively gonzo politics: Clive walking out on TV interviews, Clive hanging up on radio interviews, Jacqui Lambie calling Prime Minister Tony Abbott a "mongrel." Later, Lambie would go on an FM radio show and, when asked about her ideal man, specify "well hung" as one of the prerequisites. She was doing nothing other than playing along with the show (even though such shows get pollies on in order for them not to play along), and making a joke anyone might among friends. But the moment became another furore, with a series of pseudo-arguments about whether a man could get away with saying the opposite, decorum of parliament, etc. Lambie followed these comments up with forthright attacks on Tony Abbott and a few more phallic references – urging the government to grow a set, for instance – which further alienated her from the commentariat, who were beginning to close ranks with the major parties in regarding the PUPs as uncouth amateurs and populists. Populists maybe, or maybe not, but not particularly popular.

As the carbon-tax repeal negotiations began to stretch into week two, one began to hear, in shopping centres and at Auskick mornings, comments passed about Clive being an obstructer who was "in it for himself." News Corp was going him for, well, for everything, and for going up against Rupert – a shitzkrieg. The remainder of the press had ignored him throughout the election campaign and its aftermath, and when it was clear that he would hold the balance of power, he was judged to be motivated solely by hatred of Campbell Newman and a desire for revenge. When it came to the various Senate bills, his manoeuvring and bargaining were said to be "erratic." A reportedly aggressive and intemperate argument with the clerk of the Senate about whether or not a proposed PUP amendment was constitutional was reported as if Palmer were up on the flagpole shooting at passers-by. The objection, among the press gallery and the op-ed commentariat alike, was not so much that Palmer's policy proposals were good or bad, opportunistic or grounded in ideas, self-interested or constructive – it was simply that Palmer was there. The political media displayed the same irritation with him as they had displayed towards the Democrats and then the Greens.

Palmer had less legitimacy than either, but that was beside the point. The point was that he disturbed the orderly process of two-party politics, drip-fed to a mainstream audience (once captive, now no longer) as a wonkish battle over policy. Palmer's appearance on the scene – the contradictory process whereby a purported multi-millionaire is the means by which new and more demotic voices come into parliament – was intriguing to anyone who really loved politics, but anathema, it seemed, to those whose job was to report it.

By now, this incuriosity about Clive Palmer was starting to drive me nuts. From a standing start, at the age of sixty Clive Palmer had captured the balance of power in the nineteenth-largest economy in the world, and plonked himself in parliament for three years to do so. Was his aim merely to settle some scores with LNP enemies and protect his interests? Weren't there simpler ways to do that? Wouldn't any way be simpler than starting a political movement? With Labor and the Greens determined to play out an oppositional strategy in the Senate, Palmer had unrivalled power, for as long as he could hold sway over his basket of PUPs. Could he manage it? What did he really want? Above all, who was he?

CITIZEN CLIVE

When Clive Frederick Palmer was nine years old, he sat on the lap of Chairman Mao. True story. It was 1962, and with his parents, George and Nancy Palmer, he was in Beijing as part of a trip that would ultimately last six months. George had been running a deluxe travel agency for some years, often accompanying the tours himself and taking Nancy and young Clive with him. The selling point of George Palmer's offerings was the exotic and mysterious, in an era when travel was still a luxury for the upper middle classes, and the adventure holiday unknown.

That the Palmers visited China is not in doubt: there are photos of them walking the Great Wall, a rare privilege at a time when Red China had turned inwards and its government was stoking xenophobia against the imperialist powers that had carved up the country for so long. Was this audience with Mao a formative moment for young Clive? Did the Great Helmsman lean down and whisper in his shell-like the great phrase of the revolutionary: "There is disorder under heaven, and the situation is excellent"? Did it happen at all? Most people believe that the interview with Mao is an example of Clive's tendency to embellish a story that was already pretty good on its own, but who really knows? And if it is true, how prophetic was it of the future entrepreneur's genius for fomenting chaos and sailing through it somehow advantaged?

Whatever the case, the trip was just one of many that he would be taken on through his childhood, at an age and time when most boys would have been happy with a weekend in Bega. By the time Clive was born, in 1954, his father, George, had already had an extraordinary career, and perhaps one that could not help but frame the son's expectations of just how exciting life should be. Clive was a child of his second family, George being over fifty when Clive was born. His life reached back to an earlier era, when the country was young and an enterprising man could strike out on a path that few had travelled. George Palmer, born in 1908, had become entranced with the movies, watching silent one-reelers as a boy. So did many, but few of them at the age of fourteen, having saved enough money from being an office messenger, devoted themselves to film-making. By age sixteen, George had made a short film – of a train robbery, The Mail Robber, in the standard genre – and was touring it around halls and cinemas in Victoria, advertising himself as the "world's youngest film producer." After making a second, feature-length movie, and with a young wife and child in tow, George Palmer made it to Hollywood, where he worked as a script-writer. Returning to Australia around 1927, he moved to Tasmania and took a job in the new medium of radio, a position that introduced him to Joe Lyons, then Labor premier. Lyons went on to be prime minister, this time as leader of the United Australia Party, and George went on to be the founding manager of Melbourne radio station 3AK, before starting one of the country's first interstate bus services. Riding the bus one day, he met his second wife, Clive's mother, Nancy, then a teenager. Where George was rambunctious and restless – despite a hernia that had troubled him since the making of The Mail Robber, and which he refused to have operated on – Nancy was serious, a devout Catholic, and committed to a moral path (she had come from Tasmania to Melbourne to work in a munitions factory as part of the war effort, in case this story didn't already sound enough like an MGM classic).

When the war was over, George started his international tour company, using the spare capacity of returning ships taking new migrants to Aus-tralia, and combining it with his enduring interest in movies, of which he shot hundreds. By the mid-1950s, the Palmer family was living in Wil-liamstown in Melbourne – when they weren't cruising the world – with a thirty-metre radio tower and a home cinema. At the very beginning of the television era in Australia, while most people were marvelling at entertainment broadcast from Richmond, the Palmer family were receiv-ing programs from all over the world, catching radio waves out of the air. The Palmers had the only licensed home cinema in Australia, showing cinema releases on commercial-standard projecting equipment, with a specialisation in 3D movies (on which matter George was an advisor to the government). A news report of the family at the time – there were several – called George Palmer "the first man to see around the world."

Clive, already a budding entrepreneur selling fruit and veg in the Williamstown streets, saw New York, the world capital of business, in 1962 – the year before the China visit – at the time of the World's Fair, when a "space race" theme was filling the city with rocket toys and motifs. He saw JFK on TV, the beginning of a lifelong obsession, a leitmotif of youthful possibility. But a danger was emerging as well, as young Clive's asthma became more severe. The condition persuaded his parents, after the return from China, to move somewhere far from the old, greyish community of Williamstown.

If the Palmer family had stayed in Melbourne, Clive would be a very different person – indeed, there might not be the "Clive Palmer" we know today. But the Palmers moved to Southport, Queensland, at the top end of what is now a continuous strip, and was then a series of fishing and beach towns. The area had only been redefined the year before, by real-estate developers, as "the Gold Coast," to emphasise the notion that the area would be one of sprawl, undefined by old town boundaries. Even at this stage, the Gold Coast, and especially Surfers Paradise within it, was a place apart. Turned unashamedly towards the US and Californian glitz, it was developing tower blocks and amusement parks, and had introduced meter maids. These days it has plenty of competition, but in an Australia still oriented towards Britain, it was unique. Though the place the Palmers moved to – Rio Vista, a canal-side development inland from Southport – was hardly the land of the lotus-eaters, it was a long way from Williamstown.

Clive, underweight and frail when he arrived, shot up in adolescence to become tall, strapping and very fit (he even claimed to have once, in his twenties, outrun a horse, on a bet), which was how he would remain until he piled on vast weight after getting rich. At high school he played several sports and is remembered by friends as a relentless hatcher of plots and schemes, an organiser and ringleader, even running an "Olympics" for his friends at the time of the 1968 Mexico games – the swimming events being staged in several of the hotels that had sprung up along the coast. He founded a cricket club, sought sponsorship and qualified for the Queensland schools state athletics squad.

Still, whatever wild streak he had got from his father, whatever crazy imaginarium George Palmer had established around him, Clive's ambitions lay elsewhere: from the age of ten he wanted to be a lawyer, something his quiet, serious mother also wished for him. His parents had tried him both at Aquinas College, Queensland, and boarding at Toowoomba Grammar School, but a kid who had been round the world a number of times before the age of ten found it difficult to adjust to institutional life, and he finished his schooling at Southport State High School (even though he did not list it as his alma mater for decades) and then went up to the University of Queensland to study law in 1973. There, he appears to have faltered somewhat. Lacking the financial support of his parents – his father was by now spruiking those car-side tents that became a feature of Australian holiday sites for a couple of decades – Palmer drifted to the fringes of university life, sleeping on friends' floors, disappearing for a few weeks at a time. A steady application to the law didn't seem to be taking.

He was a member of the Liberal Party, another cause of his mother's, which was, at that stage, a viable player in Queensland politics (in the 1969 election, it had taken 23 per cent of the primary vote, compared to Coalition partner the Country Party's 21 per cent; despite that, Country Party leader Joh Bjelke-Petersen became premier, and set about reducing the Liberals to insignificance over the next two decades).

He also became involved in the anti-abortion movement, which had entered a militant phase in response to the rise of the pro-choice movement in the 1960s. In particular, Palmer became a prominent member of and spokesman for Pregnancy Now, which claimed to offer pathways out of unwanted pregnancy through adoption, child care and so on. People at the time attest to his commitment, and the many low-profile tasks he undertook, but it was an odd and at times unattractive cause, with Palmer involved in demonstrations where blown-up photos of foetuses were put garishly on display. But, of course, what could better testify to a Catholic view of the world than such a campaign? What could show greater commitment to a Catholic mother than a campaign on motherhood? At the height of his involvement, Clive led a religious march through the Gold Coast against the relaxing of abortion laws. Can you picture it, a sensibly dressed, hymn-singing crowd passing by gawping Hawaiian-shirted tourists and gold-bikini-clad meter maids? The march was as much inner journey as outer one: young Clive in yet another attempt to church his own nature.

Whatever Clive achieved by his prominent role in Pregnancy Now, it certainly distracted him from studying the law, although he remained committed to this as a career. By 1973 the wheeler-dealer in him had emerged – pulling strings, he got himself a job in the state public defender's office, with an arrangement to complete his degree in parallel. Soon, however, Palmer and another young colleague ran afoul of the Queensland police's outrageous verballing of suspects, including false confessions. Complaints about the matter got a swift result: he was transferred to the filing department, and then started getting late-night hang-up phone calls. Palmer wasn't the only person to get this treatment – the communities of coastal northern New South Wales are full of exiles from the Bjelke-Petersen years – but the menacing seemed to freak him out, and he and his girlfriend Susan (eventually to be his first wife) took off in a station wagon, not stopping till they hit Adelaide. There, Palmer became involved with the Liberal Movement, the centrist group founded by Steele Hall as a breakaway from Sir Thomas Playford's South Australian Liberal and Country League, when the latter refused to abolish the rural gerrymander that kept it in power (akin to the gerrymander that had elevated Joh Bjelke-Petersen in Queensland – where no dissent erupted).

By now, Palmer had wandered far from the law, and from the respectable and solid life he had laid out for himself, and the last vestiges went when he and Susan sold the car and bought a boat to sail up the Murray. They spent six months on the water, sometimes giving pleasure cruises to earn cash, part of the loose community of drifters and dropouts that ran up and down the river. Palmer, still fit and young, had long hair in the manner of the time, and was literally and figuratively drifting into adulthood, turning twenty-one on the water with no firm plans.

They sold the boat, bought a car and headed back to Queensland, where Palmer became involved in attempts to set up a local branch of the Liberal Movement. But the Movement's days were numbered: liberal middle-class people now mostly saw the Whitlam-led Labor Party as their political home, or else the Australia Party, which would eventually merge with the New Liberal Movement to become the Australian Democrats. And the Queensland Liberal Party was waning: 1974 was the last state election when it would outpoll the Nationals, before ultimately being absorbed by it. The Liberal Movement folded, and Clive had other things on his mind – chiefly, making a living.

He was a 21-year-old uni dropout who'd spent a few months on the dole – a time he would later recall when opposing the Abbott government's sado-conservative attempt to delay and interrupt benefits for the under-25s, saying, "I didn't know where I was going, and I needed support" – and he took a job selling real estate with a firm, N & K Projects, that specialised in packaging up land on the very edge of the Brisbane sprawl and the north Gold Coast. By his (and others') account, he sold several times his quota on the first day, racking up so many sales that prospective buyers were lined up outside the small site-office waiting to fill in their contracts, and a salesman was born. Within five years, Palmer was a real-estate sales powerhouse in his own right and a developer who was worth an estimated $40 million (estimated, it should be said, by himself).

Consolidation came quickly. Old friends were hired and became part of a burgeoning work/family tribe. He quit fooling around with progressive centrist politics and joined Joh's National Country Party. Eventually, he would track down the children from his father's first family and offer them jobs in his organisation. For a while, still in his twenties, he all but retired, and he and Susan cruised the world. Then, one day aboard the QE2, he looked around and realised that everyone else there was in their seventies. He had committed himself to a floating waiting-room for death.

Palmer's answer to this early drifting was to throw himself back into politics. But gone were the quixotic obsessions of his youth. He made an unsuccessful attempt to gain preselection for the seat of Fisher in 1984 – Peter Slipper musseled in instead – and became president of the National Party Speakers' Association and then "media director" of the party, a sop to him after controversy (he had contributed to a Labor friend's election campaign) put the party directorship out of reach. He would later say the significance of his role was exaggerated – most likely by himself at the time. His involvement in the wacky "Joh for Canberra" campaign is something now also glossed over, although the association with Joh was enough for people to enrol him in the "white shoe" brigade of coastal millionaires, such as Sanctuary Cove developer Mike Gore, who had been most prominent in the delusional push. For Palmer, however, the years of activity in the National Party were ones of consolidation: of self, life and community position.

Having set up an oil-trading partnership with a friend who was an industrial chemist, Palmer was introduced to the vast amounts of research now being pumped out of universities in the UK and Australia after the massive expansion of higher education in the 1960s and '70s. Following a UK model inaugurated by Margaret Thatcher, Palmer established Australian Commercial Research and Development (ACRD), a family-owned company designed to bundle up R&D and sell it on to the private sector. This was at a time when the idea that a university was a place of knowledge, rather than a precursor to a long chain of start-ups, still held sway, and the enterprise struggled, despite the drawing in of grandees such as Sir Mark Oliphant and Sir Frank Macfarlane Burnet to support it. But in the process, Palmer found his way to a new fortune in mining, when geologists he was working with told him about vast deposits of magnetite (a form of lower-grade iron ore) in the Pilbara, controlled by a US company, Hanna. Palmer put a deposit down to purchase the leases, and began scouring the world for buyers, a process which took him and his family to Russia for a series of *Topkapi*-style adventures.

Buyers were not found, but that proved irrelevant: Hanna had let its rights to the leases expire, and Palmer's Mineralogy snapped them up for $40,000. He had the rights, but still no buyer, and while continuing with ACRD – whose main business activity increasingly was suing former academic and government partners – and pursuing other interests, such as a Fiji casino, he would spend another two decades on the hunt for one. Along the way, he almost persuaded the New South Wales state government to pay him to build a steel refinery in Newcastle, where BHP was closing one down, and it was only in 2006 that he would be rescued by a country of his youth, China. Now that the Chinese Communist Party had delivered the greatest transition out of poverty in world history, the country's appetite for raw materials was sufficiently large that the higher-cost magnetite ore had become valuable. In 2006 a subsidiary of China's government investment company, CITIC, paid Mineralogy $415 million plus future royalties, possibly amounting to billions, for the right to mine up to six billion tonnes from Palmer's Pilbara leases.

That was the year Clive arrived. The local property baron and political insider shot into the top ten of the BRW rich list, the culmination of a process that had begun when he threw himself into real-estate sales in the 1970s. From that moment, the river-drifting hippie had been banished forever.

Forever? Well, not quite. In the year 1981, a hitherto unknown publisher, Hurricane International Press, released a slim volume called *Dreams, Hopes and Reflections*, written by F. Clive Palmer. A selection of verse on love, politics and hope inspired by the writings of Bob Dylan, John and Paul, and the life of Martin Luther King, *Dreams, Hopes and Reflections* is so redolent of its era that it may as well be wearing a Nehru jacket and listening to "Evergreen." From the bashful foreword, in which "F." tells us he was persuaded to publication only reluctantly, and that "80% of these poems were written in a single day," to the introduction by a friend – "The Honourable

Nelson Matbu, Switzerland, 1981" – DHR is a deep, deep pleasure. Matbu sounds suspiciously like Clive, even as he praises him for rescuing fallen women and wayward youth. Could they be the same person? Could they both be Peter Sellers?

In its content, DHR is exactly what you would hope for – sub-Rod McKuen-esque ("Love's Been Good to Me", "Seasons in the Sun") free verse on topics ranging from old love:

> Melanie I remember
> That day in JULY
> When we walked and talked
> Of love and peace
> Together ...

to testaments to heroes:

> Gandhi I know you
> Though I was not born
> Gandhi I know you
> Though your life was torn

to knotty philosophical reflections:

> Sand falls from
> The hourglass of life
> Sometimes before the
> Castle is finished

Which last one I would not advise the reader to contemplate stoned. The verse is no better than it ought to be, and a lot worse than it could have been, had the author spent more than a day writing it. There is no need to ignore the fact that he is currently trying to kick-start the world's largest coalmine, not exactly a Gandhian approach to the earth, our mother, but nor is there any reason to doubt the sincerity of the intent, and the clue it gives to Palmer's motives. And to his character, too, for these collected works of Clive show a degree of wilful self-deception that would serve him well in later life. The author of "Biko," about the murdered anti-apartheid activist:

> And Biko lived among us
> Gave us his life
> They cut him down
> With the knife

was a major player in a party running a government whose cops showed no compulsion about cracking open black heads for no other reason than that they were black. However he squared this, he apparently managed to do so effectively. But then, Clive may always have had a capacity for this sort of double-game. He was, after all, from and of a place where all the contradictions and possibilities of life met in one long, sandy strip.

Dog Shampooing – Massage – the Starlite Motel – the Big Golf Ball – as you zip up the Pacific Motorway, running right up the middle of the Gold Coast and into Brisbane, the pink and yellow and sky-blue and lime-green signs and hoardings fly at you, and then fly past as another set looms. Strip malls thrown up in the '80s with the chi-chi lettering of their logos and old schmicked-up '60s blocks of flats yield to canyons of towers, the older ones, meaning '70s, all but going now, dwarfed by the mega-hotels – the Chevron, the Islander – stylishly designed, here to stay, which means twenty years. Inland, the canals snake their way into what were swamps and wetlands, and the hinterland takes over – '50s and '60s homes, neat brick-veneer with a decorative twist, McMansions, the occa-sional remaining Queenslander from a time when this place was another place, low office buildings with suburban lawyers who wear Hawaiian shirts to work, crystal healing and tarot stores in tired old arcades, all of it sprawling back until the mountains begin.

Fifty kilometres long, running 10 kilometres inland from the coast, the Gold Coast is like nothing else in Australia, and not much else anywhere. One of the largest continuous "cities" in the world, it has no real centre – even the famous disarrangement of Los Angeles cannot compete with it. The Gold Coast never really rises to the level of a city. Rather, it is a sort of endless subtopia, a post-city, and thus has it been since it was created in the early 1960s.

Then, it was a series of small fishing and beach towns, a place where people came for modest holidays, mainly down from Brisbane or up from Sydney. The stretch of golden beach had been known informally as the "Gold Coast" since at least the 1930s. The small area of Elston had already been renamed "Surfers' Paradise," and in the early 1960s the upper part renamed itself the Gold Coast. By 1961, the first high-rise, "Kinkabool," had gone up (it is now heritage-listed), and others were to follow. Throughout the 1950s and into the 1960s, Surfers Paradise, the southern part of the long beach strip, had been developing as a kind of low-key mini-Miami, modest in appearance, with racy motels such as the El Dorado, restaurants such as the Hibiscus Room – known for having its own liquor licence – and a reputation for glamour and sin in an otherwise puritan and repressive state. By the 1960s, this style of development was making its way up the coast, towards Southport, hitherto an English-style beach resort, today the centre of the Gold Coast and entirely submerged within it.

As the high-rises went up along the shoreline, the land within was being transformed too. In Surfers, behind the narrow sandbar, developers began mining and dumping sand into the lagoons, to create islands ready for subdivision. Chevron Island and the Isle of Capri became sites first for homes and modest holiday developments, eventually for the towering resorts that now obscure the topography entirely. Yet at the time this was being done – with obvious disregard for the ecosystem around a network of lagoons – such feats seemed glorious. The Gold Coast was the first place where the property developer and the real-estate salesperson were rendered as heroic – in the breathless pages of its racy daily rag – and became known to the general public. Nor is it difficult to see the appeal of figures like Stanley Korman, the developer of Chevron Island, who had a near-protean ability to bring land from the water, to part the lagoons and create the promised land. Such developers were driven less by demand for more luxurious holidays – Australians continued to see a beach holiday as something much closer to nature, with a touch of the pioneer spirit, of roughing it in shacks and spending all day at the beach – than they were by the sheer desire to build it, and create the demand.

In doing so, they created a thought-bridge to America, speeding along our identification with a way of life and a set of cultural values far more unlike ours than would come to be seen to be the case. Queensland's territorial imagination had been dominated by its vast dry stretches, its resistant land and parching heat. The Gold Coast, its timber and sugarcane days long gone, was its simple opposite: a watery fantasia, where land had to be created, not tamed. It was equally contrary in its morality. Surfers and the Gold Coast were not only more fun than Queensland, a state that banned men's magazines, censored mainstream films and banned sex education, even into the '80s – they were more fun than the rest of Australia, a place of early closing and bad restaurants. On the Gold Coast there were nitespots and cabaret acts, fine dining and free-flowing liquor, "pyjama parties" in the motels, gangsters up from Sydney for a good time, international stars from Lauren Bacall to Lee Marvin, and a conveyor belt from triumph to disgrace and prison for the developers extending the new megalopolis in every direction.

By the late 1960s, the Gold Coast was more than simply an anomaly within the state. Its creation of value *ab nihilo*, in rezoning, reclaiming and developing, had come to be central to the state's prosperity. The Gold Coast roared ahead, in a state whose dependency on rural production had put it into a decades-long decline. Furthermore, the Coast itself had become a site for the intersection of different forms of capital, with developers, real-estate packagers, politicians, vacationing miners, organised crime bosses and foreign investors coming into close proximity, and then being intertwined in ever more ambitious deals, combining property with entertainment.

The Gold Coast provided the means by which Brisbane, a large country town until the 1970s, would become a developer's boomtown and a conduit for increasing amounts of Japanese investment, at a time when the land of the rising sun was widely seen as a half-sinister force, intent on world domination. For Queensland's Coalition government, led by Country Party leaders rather than the Liberal Party, the influx of such new money was divisive from the start, separating the party elite from its membership. The latter remained nativist, rural and nationalist, economically and otherwise. They believed the Country Party to be the guardians of their values, when in fact the party – in sync with its name-change to the National Country Party in 1975 and then the National Party of Australia in 1982 – was becoming an efficient vehicle for corruption on a vast scale, with the boosting of coastal development one of its key functions.

The hot centre of the Gold Coast could thus only operate as an excluded zone – it was Queensland and not-Queensland, where hedonism, fancy and fantasy, rootlessness, held sway in a state ruled over by a literalist Lutheran, amid powerful mythologies of ceaseless hard work among God's bounty. Yet many of those who would come to make their fortunes on the Coast would see the fantasia they had created as, in the last analysis, an expression of that ethic. Had they not brought something out of nothing? Was that not the principle by which Christianity and capitalism met? The first developers of the Gold Coast were cheerful pirates; those who came later, when the place became a long ribbon of towers, arcades and gallerias, had a more serious view of their activities and their place in society. Their financial interests were tied up in a regime that minimised property tax, explicitly and implicitly subsidised development, and restricted trade union activity.

Though the style of the Gold Coast was at variance with the more strait-laced state that played host to it, there was, at root, a unity. Queensland's status as the last frontier, the only verdant state where free land could be carved out of the bush, had an echo in the Gold Coast's radical self-invention. This sprawling post-urban space, purposefully exceeding any fixed notion of a city, and mining its own beaches to make islands, was a frontier within, a place which prized individuality above all, not least in its planning laws. The Gold Coast was different from Queensland, but Queensland was different from Australia, and from its depths unique creatures came. Was it the heat? Was it the distance? The remoteness? Whatever the case, the things that came out of Queensland could come from nowhere else in the country.

Over the decades, considerable ink has been spilt debating the nature of "Queensland exceptionalism," but there is widespread agreement on certain factors. The first is provincialism, as a political-economic and cultural factor: development in the region/colony/state was always more oriented to rural centres than to the distant capital, due to distance and a strong reliance on agriculture and the small-farm sector. Queensland Labor, alone of the Labor parties, focused on rural workers and communities, and succeeded in dominating the state's politics for the first half of the twentieth century. The party had arisen from the shearers' strikes of the 1890s, and Queensland remained a byword for left radicalism right into the 1950s, with the Communist Party playing a major role in north Queensland politics in the inter-war period. In the late 1940s, the state elected Australia's only Communist MP, Fred Paterson.

Such left radicalism produced a reaction, and from World War I on, the state was a crucible for the right-wing populist politics of the era. It flourished for the same reason that right-wing populism flourishes everywhere: small farmers felt themselves to be powerless with regard to changing commodity prices, interest rates and the like, all dictated from the metropolitan centres. Queensland was the only place in Australia where the inter-war "social credit" movement flourished – a corporatist proposal whereby all "productive" citizens were held to be shareholders in the economy, and thus deserving of a social dividend. In the post-war period, social credit would flow into the toxic politics of the anti-Semitic League of Rights, which found great success in the north – numbering among its adherents the future Liberal grandee James Killen.

The far-flung state was amenable to populist views for cultural reasons as well. Both sides of politics made a virtue of simple rural life, underfunding urban development, industry and education for decades on end. Among family-based farming communities, evangelical religion boomed, with the state the home of the travelling tent show. In the south of the state, the long-term presence of an Italian migrant community gave conservative Catholicism a social base. For much of the twentieth century, the state was in a slow decline due to diminishing demand for agricultural products, thus adding to a sense that a whole way of life was being undermined by powerful forces beyond. When the bumpkin MP – thus was he seen by colleagues – Joh Bjelke-Petersen became premier in 1968, the Country Party had a figure who could draw on populist energies to gain solid majority support.

Bjelke-Petersen was both figurehead and leader, surrounded by a cabal of politicians who turned the state's politics away from bucolic rural idylls and focused it on coastal development and mining. While this was under-way, Bjelke-Petersen's backwoods manner provided the ideal cover for the transformation of Queensland. Throughout the 1970s and 1980s, as politi-cal affiliation began to develop a cultural dimension – was so and so a real Queenslander/Aussie, or was she/he a "trendy"? – the National Party managed to take over a section of the Labor vote (the continued rural gerry-mander – first introduced by Labor – helped here) and fashion itself as the true opposition to the Whitlam, Hawke and, indeed, Fraser governments. Joh's achievement, culminating in the delusional "Joh for Canberra" push, was to offer an ostensible resistance to modernity, while simultaneously encouraging its spread through unfettered development. Over and above that, he hammered the trendies on the environment, social issues and race.

Race is the dimension of Queensland exceptionalism and populism most often passed over, but it provides the focus for the movement's obses-sional nature, and hence its ceaseless return. In an imperial era, Queens-land felt itself to be a triple-frontier – against Aboriginal Australians, who put up a decades-long struggle against the theft of their lands for pastoral grazing; against Asia, on its doorstep; and against Pacific Islanders, who had been pressed into service halfway between indentured labour and de facto slavery. The perceived need for racial purity, and the ever-present threat of its dissolution, gave a concrete form to more abstract notions of powerful forces behind the scenes, controlling everyday life.

The Bjelke-Petersen government achieved the difficult manoeuvre of becoming the representative of such populism, at the same time as it was opening the door to Asian property investors on a grand scale, and it achieved this largely by resisting all federal attempts to improve the lot of Aboriginal Australians, and by ruthlessly oppressing any internal activism by Queensland Aboriginal groups. But racial and xenophobic fears were buried too deep in the political culture to be fully abolished. When they returned, they would come not only from the heartland, but also from the coastal sprawl that had, in the intervening decades, become the state's new centre.

Queensland populism and the Gold Coast model of what one might call "sprawl politics" came together with the rise of Pauline Hanson and the One Nation "movement." Hanson, the fish-and-chip shop owner who had been disendorsed by the Liberal Party in the lead-up to the 1996 federal election, was from Ipswich, a town about as far from the Gold Coast sensibility as one could imagine. The place was old, industrial, showing no particular regard for the lush subtropical region in which it found itself. When Hanson decided to contest Oxley, without Liberal Party support – in what was assumed to be a safe Labor seat – she gained a massive 21 per cent swing and found herself in parliament.

The victory surprised her as much as anyone, as did the thunderous national reaction to her maiden speech, which gained mass support (and mass opposition) for its attack on multiculturalism and Asian immigration and its warning of dark times ahead. Hanson later said that she was swamped by the process, and it was at this point that groups of supporters began spontaneously to coalesce. The Pauline Hanson Support Movement, formed by the aptly named Bruce Whiteside, found an early home on the Gold Coast, with much of its most vocal support coming from prosperous retirees and sun-changers, who'd moved north for both the natural climate and the business one (low taxes and minimised regulations). The movement, with a lot of internal argy-bargy, would eventually become One Nation. Months after Hanson's victory and maiden speech, a poll showed she was attracting a potential primary vote of 18 per cent. In the Queensland election of 1998, the party took eleven seats.

Later, it would be revealed that there was no party at all, and that the movement had been hijacked – and partly created – by the carpetbaggers who gathered round Hanson after her surprise victory, the "party" being a two-man-owned private corporation, with "members" in fact signing up to an ancillary group with no power of party direction. Perhaps that was as "Gold Coast" as a populist movement gets – where even something purporting to represent the "will of the people" is a shonky pyramid scheme. Even in 1998, One Nation was riven with internal divisions and splits, and by the 2009 state election it had disappeared entirely.

Hanson's first visible intervention in 1996 – a letter to the paper accusing Australian politicians of causing "a racism problem" by showering Aborigines "with money, facilities and opportunities that only these people can obtain" – was mild by today's standards (and by comparison with some of the things she would say in the days before and after her election), and much of it came to be incorporated into Liberal Party policy, or at least rhetoric. Her populism had a peculiarly Queensland character in its obsession with race and the defence of whiteness: in a telling slip, she made one high-profile speech in which she worried that "blood would be split" – she meant to say "spilt." The mask of civic concern that populism paraded under slipped a little.

In other ways, however, Hanson was tapping into a light version of the populism that John Howard had unleashed on his return to the opposition leadership in 1995, with a campaign against political correctness and rule by "the elite." This importation of the US culture wars was designed to shift the basis of political allegiance and make it possible for Howard to scoop up substantial votes of one-time rusted-on Labor supporters, dismayed by economic restructuring, Paul Keating's frolics into history and the arts, and the changing culture of a place where Anglo-Celtic society was losing its absolute centrality. Yet Hanson's politics also contained a great deal of economic nationalism and corporatism, policies which found great favour in rural and regional Queensland, and which were not to be satisfied by the Howard government's steady neoliberalisation of the economy.

By the mid-2000s, with Hanson now a professional TV special guest and serial electoral-funding welfare queen, populism in Queensland was shifting back to its rural heartland. In this fraught period, Hanson gained some collateral support from Bob Katter, the member for the far north Queensland seat of Kennedy, a man with a taste for white stetson hats and gold cufflinks, who complained of the "slanty-eyed ideologues" attacking his colleague Bob Burgess, after Burgess had called citizenship ceremonies "dewoggings." Katter claimed his phrase was an old one, akin to "pointy-headed intellectuals," but it was racially charged enough to ring alarm bells.

For many southerners, this outburst was the first they'd heard of Katter, a state and then federal MP whose father had been a legendary figure in Queensland politics. They were soon to hear a lot more. Throughout the 2000s Katter became ever more displeased with what he saw as a raw deal for rural Australia. As the National Party's influence waned within the Coalition, and agriculture continued to diminish as a share of the Australian economy, the old Liberal–National, city–country compact was coming apart. Katter was vocal about his discontents, and in 2001 he broke away altogether, first sitting as an independent and then forming Katter's Australia Party. The move out of the National Party framework gave Katter more independence on economic matters and less restraint on social ones. That quickly created problems for him. Though socially conservative himself – he was famous for having organised a protest against the Beatles in 1964, arguing that the screaming teenagers who greeted them in Brisbane were being seduced by "idolatry" – like most professional politicians he had long since accepted that we lived in a cosmopolitan and diverse world, and his principal focus was economic neglect of the regions. But many of his most fervent organisers were less comfortable and relaxed about contemporary Australia, and Katter's Australia Party soon became entangled in debates about same-sex marriage and safe-injecting rooms in Sydney, which did not seem the most pressing issues facing dying rural towns.

By the time Katter got his show on the road, he'd been joined by another rural figure: Barnaby Joyce, National Party senator, elected in 2004. Joyce was an accountant from Tamworth who had moved to St George in western Queensland, a strong Catholic heartland, and he was a conservative Catholic himself. From the start he made it clear that he would regard the Coalition whip as strictly provisional and would act on his conscience and with reference to the particular interests of his region. With his proud country schnozz and slightly squat appearance, Joyce cut an interesting figure in the new

parliament. Knowingly or otherwise, he played up to a Mr. Smith Goes to Washington image, at one point lamenting the loneliness of the nation's capital and
wondering if it would be possible for senators to meet and vote online from
the regions in which they lived. By 2007 he was beginning to talk more
broadly about matters global and financial.

In the wake of the 2008 financial crisis, and the use of stimulus budgeting and quantitative easing, the complex and fabricated nature of global
capitalism became an issue of concern to many. In the US, Ron Paul had
built a movement out of opposition to financialisation and the big banks,
in the name of "real" notions of value, corresponding to small-scale
enterprise and labour. Paul's movement was riddled with racism, anti-
Semitism and wild-eyed conspiracy, all of which he was lax about repu-
diating, but its core appeal was the notion that collapse and malaise had
come about because of the original sin of central banking.

By late 2009 Joyce was drawing on some of that sentiment, warning of
funny money and a possible US default. He was sowing seeds in fertile
soil, that cultivated for decades in rural areas by the Australian League of
Rights, and tapping into the powerlessness that peripheral communities
dependent on the shifting returns of agriculture often feel towards the
City. He harked back to conservative Catholic attitudes to money, debt and
value, even using the term "usury" to describe the modern financial system.
Opposition leader Tony Abbott's response to this meddlesome priestliness
was to make Joyce his shadow finance minister, sacrificing a brief loss of
credibility for Joyce's rapid and inevitable self-destruction in the role.

Whether Joyce ever gained much of a groundswell of support for his
crusade is doubtful, but for students of obscure movements it was deli-
cious indeed, a direct link from the present to the distant, sepia-shrouded
'20s and '30s, the era of social credit and the "money power." With Joyce
muzzled, and then making a move to the lower house en route to party
leadership (the party currently has no leader, using the name "Warren
Truss" on official forms, in the same way morgues tag unidentified
corpses "John Doe"), Bob Katter appeared to have the populist field to

himself. He prepared to run a full slate of candidates, and expected to pick up a Senate seat in Queensland, and thus have a stake in the balance of power. By the beginning of 2013, the media were gradually adjusting to the idea that the Senate race would be ... interesting, and driven by popular dissatisfaction with the major parties.

And then, in late April 2013, Clive Palmer stood before a banana-yellow scrim to announce that he had formed a political party, which would be fielding a full list of candidates in the 2013 federal election.

For all but the most seasoned political observers, Palmer's entry into the political sweepstakes came as a surprise. But it had been brewing for nearly two years, the product of a brutal rift between Palmer and the new Queensland premier, Campbell Newman, a rift that involved a split between the parliamentary and organisational wings of the LNP. For years, Palmer's power within the party, such as it was, had been based on the latter wing, and buttressed by generous donations. But the party was in part a victim of its own success. After years in opposition, and with more than a decade of bitter conflict before the Liberal and National parties united in the LNP, the mammoth 2012 state election victory gave the parliamentary wing a disastrous hubris. The Newman government brought down a budget pushing the state towards immediate surplus, and sacking 10,000 public servants into the bargain. The move brought immediate protest from Palmer, known as a more centrist figure than many in the party.

Of more immediate concern was the Newman cabal's move to end public funding for party administration, dealing Labor a kick in the guts while also undermining the power of the administrative wing of the LNP. To rub it in, the Newman government turned a deaf ear to all requests for special consideration in getting Clive's massive Galilee Basin project underway. There were also mutterings that Clive's son, Michael Palmer, had been selected and then deselected for a state seat. Open criticism of the Newman government by Palmer degenerated into warfare, with the parliamentary wing trying to head off a departure by Palmer, worried that he would be able to hive off members of the LNP parliamentary party and create a new party with sufficient numbers to constitute itself as the opposition, as opposed to beleaguered Labor, with its mere seven parliamentary members.

That didn't happen: Palmer nabbed only two LNP members, Alex Douglas and Carl Judge – both of whom would eventually leave PUP in 2014 – and quietly registered the name "United Australia Party" in the weeks before that morning in April 2013 when he announced the formation of his new outfit. However, the Australian Electoral Commission ruled that the name was too similar to that of another party and so, with reluctance and deep humility on Clive's part, the name was changed to the Palmer United Party within the first month.

Most people dismissed it out of hand as a quixotic gesture by an eccentric plutocrat, little recognised outside the state or even within it. With its branded name, the PUP sounded like a Katter imitation, everyone agreeing that Bob was the main game in town – a man and a party with a real social base, detaching from the Nationals after many decades of diminishing returns.

By contrast, in his white shirt and pinstripe blue suit, Clive had no trace of the rural about him. His principal cause was to repeal and refund the carbon tax, self-interest presented as a mass cause. On refugees – a test-case for the charge of populism, if ever there was one – he was more compassionate than the other parties and, indeed, than what the public demanded. He had a lot of guff about love and revolution, and he twerked in radio studios. That was about it. Yet this was sufficient for Palmer to be enrolled, in the public mind and by the press, in the great tradition of Queensland populism. He was seen as drawing on a heartland, and a myth of it, that he had no relationship with at all. When I told a well-known literary critic that Clive had authored a volume of poetry, he guessed it would resemble bad Banjo Patterson, with long lines of pastoral balladeering, rhyming and scanning. It was nothing of the sort, of course, as we have seen – indeed, exactly the opposite, loose and FM radio-y, a product of '60s-era suburban universality. But the misapprehension captured a widespread assumption, based in part on the way, in the "Joh for Canberra" and Pauline Hanson years, the rural populist tradition had mingled with the new world of coastal economic development.

Clive Palmer was no backcountry rural populist. He was, first and foremost, a man of the Coast – the Gold Coast – formed as a boy by it, prospering within it, steeped deeply in its ethos and attitude, perhaps despite his best wishes not to be. When your neighbours are five-star hotels, porpoise aquariums, groovy nitespots and hot-sheet motor-inns, you're going to have different expectations of life, and different habits of thought, to the average Joe. When you start to make your fortune, and find your vocation, in selling the real estate that will extend the city and build it, then you are imbued not with the sense of struggle and resentment essential to rural populism, but instead with a feeling of possibility and transformation. The world is not the resistant and unforgiving earth, or the hard silver coins of the bankers, but a place which can be made and remade at will, a world with a porous boundary of fantasy and reality. Palmer's rise represented the full disentanglement of coastal Queensland from rural Queensland. True, he captured many of the inland votes that would otherwise have gone to Bob Katter – on the trail with the Kat in the hat in 2013, I witnessed the man pull up at the roadside and more or less weep with frustration at Clive's vastly greater amount of signage – but they were just coming along for the ride. Unlike Katter, Clive never campaigned on nativist issues, and his refugee policy was out in the open for all to see. Palmer was the Sunshine Coast, rising. Such regions did not, in themselves, constitute a base. But they didn't need to. Thanks to a few kinks in the system, Palmer's fantasy would become our reality.

Yet, as fantasies go, it was not without content. Beyond the obvious agendas of his business interests, score-settling and need for attention, there was a centrist core to Palmer's politics that appeared to arise from his religious upbringing. It was easy to miss beneath the clowning, as many in the mainstream media were only too willing to demonstrate.

There's something piquant about Clive Palmer owning a golf course, for the resemblance between His Cliveness and Rodney Dangerfield in *Caddyshack* seems more than coincidental. Wandering across the greens, bug-eyed, paunchy and badly dressed, with a gaggle of Chinese investors in tow, he don't get no respect.

From the moment Palmer launched his party, the mainstream press was sniffy, the *Australian* calling him a "political fringe-dweller" with "relevance deprivation syndrome" (27 April 2013), while for some weeks Fairfax refused to acknowledge him at all, until a profile in *Good Weekend* noted that he was playing the fool in order to gain a slew of "uncritical airplay" (20 July 2013). Apart from that, the *Age* and the SMH largely ignored him, while the *Australian* – slowly realising that Palmer might constitute a threat to the coming Abbott hegemony – kept up a withering barrage, reporting on the disendorsement of a West Australian candidate, a tirade against Chinese business executives, a lawsuit over his soccer interests, some brief reports on his taxation policy and ad spending, and Palmer's accusations that Tony Abbott had sabotaged his plane. Only when the election campaign reached its final week was there coverage with some political substance: a profile in the *Sunday Age*, which cast a critical eye over Palmer's spending promises and wondered if his campaign was all a huge joke (1 September 2013), along with a stray report on the possibility that Glenn Lazarus, polling at 8 per cent, might get over the line. The *Australian* dutifully noted Palmer's accusation that Wendi Deng was a Chinese spy, but its long overview of the prospects of the minor parties in the Senate mentioned only Lazarus as a chance, and never entertained the possibility that the PUP would hold the balance of power (5 September 2013).

Unsurprisingly, that disdain changed in the days following the election, as per the *Australian*'s article "I'm Kingmaker" (9 September 2013), describing Palmer's victory as "stunning" and the PUP as a "come-from-nowhere party." A story added helpfully the next day, "He's hard to miss but the

LNP never saw Clive Palmer coming." They weren't the only ones. Fairfax's headline to a news story speculating, as the votes were being counted, that Palmer might lose the seat of Fairfax but end up with three senators was the snarky "Palmer satisfied with having sold Australia a PUP" (15 September 2013). For its part, from the end of the election to April Fools Day 2014, the *Australian* published more than three hundred articles on Palmer's business dealings, his Senate negotiations, his quoting of Chairman Mao in his maiden speech, and the peasant uprising by villa holders at the Coolum resort, whom he was trying to starve out, but next to nothing resembling an opinion piece on the PUP's policies or stated intentions. At Fairfax, they were more even-handed, but no less bemused. Mark Kenny covered Palmer's threat to white-ant Abbott's carbon-tax repeal, but had little to offer on the PUP's politics as they were beginning to emerge, noting only that "Big Clive is no ideologue" and that parties based around single personalities rarely last (25 April 2014). It was only when Palmer appeared with Al Gore in the Great Hall of Parliament House on 23 June and announced that he was a global warming convert and would be loading the abolition of the carbon tax with conditions that Fairfax began to contemplate some analysis of his beliefs and motives.

The *Australian* was more forensic, and exhaustive, in its analysis of Clive's dealings, but it wavered between rational assessment of just how bad things were being made for the Coalition and sheer exasperation. Philip Hudson (30 June 2014) endorsed Victorian Liberal MP Kelly O'Dwyer's comment that, on climate change, "Clive's got more positions than the *Kama Sutra*," while Peter van Onselen (7 June 2014) offered calmer advice in perhaps the worst written sentence since the composing of "The Battle of Maldon": "Undoubtedly the antics of team Palmer will create an optical illusion of a circus, an appearance the media will focus on."

What no one in the commentariat or press gallery had, however, was any analysis or interpretation of Palmer as a political force, with an integrated set of beliefs, however dishonoured they might be in the breach. That was a significant omission before the new Senate met; by the time it was in session, it was an un-ignorable one. Palmer's thwarting of the Abbott government's last hopes for a winter/spring session with a few wins, his vociferous attack on the proposed Medicare co-payment and the new arrangements for unemployed youth, his opposition to the government's privatisation booster, and his refusal to allow through the repeal of the mining tax if it also meant the abolition of the social welfare measures attached to it – none of this registered with the commentariat as a consistent body of beliefs. When Palmer appeared at a National Press Club lunch in the second week of the Senate sitting and reiterated his commitment to these policies, it was judged by Tony Wright in the *Age* (8 July 2014) as merely an aggrieved response to the sudden attention the PUP senators were receiving in their own right.

"If Clive Palmer and his merry band of senators have a grand plan for what they hope to achieve in this, the 44th Parliament, it is difficult to see what that may be," intoned an *Age* editorial on 9 July. In the *Sydney Morning Herald* (8 July 2014), Mark Kenny found Palmer "chaotic" – even though much of what he took to be inconsistency was down to procedure: PUP support for Direct Action, for example, was now inevitable because Abbott had put it in the budget core. (Palmer would eventually announce that he had come to an agreement with the government to pass Direct Action, in exchange for keeping open the possibility of an emissions trading scheme, by means of an inquiry to be headed by Bernie Fraser. It was another fancy move by the dealmaker, with a little help from his friends.)

While Fairfax remained bewildered, News Corp's fury only mounted. By Bastille Day, the *Australian*'s Philip Hudson was in tumbrel mood, demanding Palmer agree to the axing of the carbon tax immediately, because a Newspoll sampling had suggested a majority of voters wanted him to. Week by week, Hedley Thomas's investigation into the CITIC–Mineralogy deal ticked over. And there was a full court press from the commentators, with an unmistakable tone of bitterness seeping in – as in government loyalist Niki Savva's thousand-plus-word tirade (17 July 2014). Abbott was anxious not to antagonise Palmer, she said – "as if it's possible to woo a brown snake". Right up to the time of writing, as the Palmer and PUP incidents piled up – from guru-for-hire Deepak Chopra complaining of the facilities at the Coolum resort, to Jacqui Lambie's claim that she was part-Aboriginal and sent to the Senate by God – News Corp played it for laughs while also seeking to discredit Palmer utterly. Fairfax simply shrugged its shoulders – as though Palmer were part of a world it didn't understand anymore, one where its brand of journalism could find no purchase.

Throughout July, with some interest I observed the consensus on Palmer emerge. Having missed much of his antics in the first half of the year, I was getting up to speed. I read Clive, Sean Parnell's 2013 biography (his findings form the basis for my reflections on Palmer's life here) and gained a picture of a more complex man than the reportage had suggested, and watched as he put the government through hell in the Senate. This was the point at which I began to notice a serious divergence between what I was seeing and what the press gallery was reporting. For me, Palmer's manoeuvres were politics of the sort on display every day in forums such as the US Congress: bluff, horse-trading and deals going on and off the table in pursuit of your interests, of those of your constituents and even of your ideas about how the world might be better. Maybe it's the best way to do things, maybe not, but it is certainly politics.

But not to the Australian commentariat, for whom the disarray was a sign of the end-times. The prospect of a house of parliament being a genuine forum, in which a majority had to be actually made and kept, and remade for each new bill, gave the press a bad case of the vapours. They appeared unable to see that alongside Palmer's buffoonery – some of it done for a sort of zen koan effect, some of it simply an expression of the man's nature – a real political process was taking place.

Nor was there much consistency in the suggestion of Palmer's inconsistency. From the moment I first saw him – at the Coolum Resort open day – Palmer had been banging on about the unfairness of the Abbott government's budget. He had also made clear his opposition to the crazy dole plans for the young, and to an increase in university fees. He didn't waver from this. He hasn't, at time of writing. While Labor went mealy-mouthed over much of the budget – conscious that some of the free-mouseketeers at its heart had suggested a Medicare co-payment and dole sequestering years earlier – Palmer made bold statements about right and wrong, and what Australians owed to each other. This was buttressed by his argument – supported by economists across the spectrum – that there was no budget emergency, that we had a low deficit and a manageable debt, and that underinvestment in an era of cheap money would be more costly in the long run than servicing the obligations we now had.

Palmer seemed to be being judged by a standard not only harsher than that applied to others, but also plainly contradictory. It was, after all, the Abbott government that had been utterly inconsistent, which is to say lying, in bringing down a budget with a raft of measures it had ruled out in the preceding election campaign. When the PUP and other parties scrambled to find a response to these surprise measures, they were accused of making it up on the fly. Equally, the commentariat couldn't decide whether to hate Palmer for being intransigent, despite the shaky legitimacy of his vote, or for making deals that got legislation through. The latter disdain was the most fantastic of all, since it set itself against the idea implicit in the bicameral system: that the upper house should review legislation but ultimately show regard for the fact that the public had chosen a government, with a program, in the lower house. Palmer and the PUPs' behaviour here was consistent with that spirit – they made deals to let through the legislation, the carbon and mining tax repeals – as they had always said they would – which the government had cam-paigned on, and came to a deal regarding the amendments attached to them for which the government could not claim a mandate. This was surely bicamerality working as intended. A huge fuss was made over the fact that the PUP had put a guillotine on the schoolkids bonus and the low-income superannuation contribution attached to the mining tax, pre-serving them only for the life of this parliament. But that was surely part of a deal, of getting to yes, while preserving the measures for the life of the parliament – such that Labor could campaign on their retention if it wanted – and hardly a flat sell-out.

That the PUP was a motley crew, slammed together through circumstance, was not in dispute. Nor was it in dispute that Palmer ruled it like a fiefdom, in some consultation with Lazarus, and less so with the other two senators – a source of growing irritation to Jacqui Lambie. But after delving back into Palmer's past, via Parnell, and matching it up with his current policies and pronouncements, it seemed clear to me who Palmer was and where he was coming from. Whatever ludicrously self-interested measures he might introduce – such as the inquiry into the Newman government, his arch-nemesis – there was unquestionably a commitment to a certain worldview, which might be of interest to know.

But no one I encountered, it seemed, had read Sean Parnell's biography of Palmer – save for Clive's new *eminence verte*, the Australia Institute's Ben Oquist, who told me he had grabbed the book as soon as it came out. It seemed that some, at least, were trying to work out what Clive Palmer's intentions were, and whether he came in peace.

"I was hunting for fishies!" a four-year-old Clive Palmer said, as he was coaxed back through the porthole, having climbed out onto a thin ledge running around the Dutch freighter on which the Palmer family were travelling. Having resisted attempts by the crew to haul him in ("You get away from me!"), Clive had finally been persuaded by his mother that he had something on his back.

Decades later, the anecdote, printed at the time in the *Women's Weekly*, resurfaced and was passed around, to general amazement, even though it had already been retold in Parnell's biography. For many it captured young Palmer: bumptious, foolish, easily distracted, lacking common sense.

Simultaneously, there was another story being told, as Hedley Thomas's investigations continued their remorseless advance. Palmer was a shonk, a flim-flam guy. There was no shortage of corroborating evidence for that view. By 2008 Palmer's involvement with the Queensland National and Liberal parties had become all-embracing, with a donation of nearly half a million dollars, and an emergency donation of $100,000 given to the Liberals to save them from bankruptcy. When the Nationals finally absorbed the Liberals and became the LNP, Palmer was accused of having bought a party.

In parallel, his business interests had expanded to take in nickel and cobalt, the Gold Coast United soccer team, the Coolum resort, a project to rebuild the *Titanic* (because that design worked so well the last time), and above all a company called Waratah Coal, which had large reserves in the Galilee Basin which it could not get out, with no rail-line to the coast, and no authorisation to create a port on the Great Barrier Reef. By the time Anna Bligh's Labor government passed into history, the Waratah project had become China First, a massive partnership to mine the Galilee Basin and move the coal by rail 310 kilometres north to a new port at Abbot Point, the project potentially worth tens of billions of dollars.

Palmer had been instrumental in the manoeuvres to make Campbell Newman the premier of Queensland, so when the new government turned round and downgraded the "major project" status of the Galilee Basin / Abbot Point project, and backed a rival rail project into the bargain, Palmer went on the attack against the party that had made him its youngest ever life member. His initial feint was to make a large donation to the "Hope Fund" of Together, the Queensland public sector union that was fighting the large public sector cuts by Newman, and to criticise what he argued was an unnecessary and cruel austerity policy, at a time when growth was required. The party infighting did not subside; the China First project did not get the sort of support that Palmer wanted for it, and in late 2012, after some negotiations about quitting or being expelled, he left the party of which he was a life member. After a gap of a few months, he launched the outfit which would soon bear his name.

To anyone who had been following the LNP's internal feudings – which was not many, outside Queensland – the motives for Palmer's launch into brand-name politics were obvious. Having failed to split the LNP and form a new party with sitting members, he was entering federal parliament as a pincer movement against Campbell Newman – an accusation borne out by his subsequent success in having the Senate launch an inquiry into the Queensland government. Others suggested that it was only ever about getting the Galilee Basin project moving by any means necessary. Still yet a third interpretation was that Clive had gone a bit mad, and that this massive political endeavour was him off on a frolic of his own.

By the time these three explanations had travelled a distance, intertwining and coming apart again, I'd spent a few months watching Clive in action, reading his backstory, trying to think ahead of his latest stunt. Increasingly, I began to wonder if we were seeing the same person. Whatever and whoever Clive Palmer was, he wasn't a simple man, and his desires were not easily interpretable, even to himself. His standing up for the common folk was not always principled, naturally, but his apparent venality was not always selfish. If he was building a populist outfit to win over old culturally right-wing Labor voters and "cut the crap" Liberal ones, he was going about it in a pretty bloody funny way, standing next to Al Gore and taking on a greenish hue, thus pissing off Queensland Laborites, while holding the line against Hockey's fiscally conservative, punishing budget. He took on the colours of economic nationalism, yet suggested we buy our submarines overseas because it was cheaper and better to do so. He was in politics for the big carve-up, apparently, yet he rejected the assets-recycling program. He was after the anti-politics vote, yet he talked down Jacqui Lambie's ignorant conflation of religious laws with the laws of the land. None of it, by the test of self-interest, made a blind bit of sense, taken as a whole. Yet immediate self-interest was the line people stuck to, because it fitted an easy narrative and gave shape to a quickly written news report. By contrast, if you assumed that Palmer was a complex man, rather than a simple one, and that his political actions worked off a consistent set of beliefs, rather than as mere diversions and pandering, things fell somewhat into place. Such a view of Clive was also one that cut with the grain of Australian political history.

Who is Clive Palmer? He's a man so utterly a creation of the Gold Coast that you can smell the coconut oil and sand on him, but he's also an observant Catholic whose public statements have the timbre of religious tradition about them. He's a man who wanted to be a lawyer and a stable man of the establishment, but found that his truer nature as a natural-born salesman and wheeler-dealer would win out in the end. He's a long-time associate of the Queensland LNP, an outfit that was an enabler of racist brutality for decades, yet he wrote a poem lamenting the murder of Steve Biko. He's a relentless builder of empires, however flimsy, whose life appears to have been genuinely influenced by the countercultural currents of the '60s. He's a man who speaks of a love revolution, then sues everybody. He contains multitudes, which explains the amplitude and the waddle. These conflicting tendencies are held together with a tad less calm integration than he would wish for, of which more in a bit, but for the moment it is worth considering that the politics of Clive Palmer, whatever personal vendettas and agendas may be being exercised through them, are exactly what they claim to be: a mildly centre-right politics, grounded in Australian Catholic traditions and social movement doctrine, and tracing their lineage back to the party whose name he wanted to adopt, the United Australia Party.

In this respect, Palmer's objective politics tap into his personal history – his father's friendship with, and role as informal advisor to, Catholic centrist politician Joe Lyons, and his mother's commitment to, and communication of, a serious Catholicism, with its notion of service in the world. Palmer's first way of bearing witness to that commitment was in a relatively fraught and ostentatious form, as part of the aggressive Right to Life campaigns of the early 1970s, a movement he now leaves off his CV. It's an embarrassing item, to be sure, but perhaps he is also genuinely ashamed of Right to Life's merciless and persecutory style; he has continued to play up his involvement in Pregnancy Now, and his departure when it began to drift into a pure anti-abortion mode.

Likewise his involvement with the Liberal Movement in the mid-1970s: doubtless it arose in part from a desire to help build a group that could damage the party that had put him on the run from Queensland. But it was scarcely a move indicative of someone with clear-eyed and wholly personal ambition; the Liberal Movement was doomed to be a small player from the start, never with the prospect of government, and to join it was to choose a path to irrelevance. But it was the principal expression of a liberal centrist urge in the mid-1970s, until the Democrats were formed, partly from its ruins.

The policies that Palmer urges now – which oppose harsh budgeting that targets the poor, which see the state, capital and labour as engaged in a triple partnership, which reflect a belief that further privatisations would be a betrayal of our common holdings, and take a Keynesian and demand-driven attitude to deficit and public debt – these are nothing other than the centre-right politics that determined the position of the non-Labor parties from the formation of the UAP in 1931, and carried right through, including into much of the Howard/Costello era. Indeed, this long period was bookended by two similar events: the Nationalists' attempt to kill the arbitration system in the late 1920s, and the subsequent election of the Scullin government in 1929; and John Howard's hubristic introduction of WorkChoices in 2005, and his subsequent election loss at the height of a boom. Because the arbitration system and the Harvester judgment that inaugurated it took their moral language from *Rerum Novarum*, the 1891 encyclical that sparked off the Catholic social movements, we can say that it is this doctrine, and its secular variants, that sits at the very centre of Australian political values, and major parties depart too far from it at their peril. It consists not merely of a set of social rules, but of an idea of what it is to be human, an idea of depth, and of selfhood as achieved in the exercise of mutual obligation. Such a doctrine, drawing also from nineteenth-century social liberalism and classical and Christian notions of freedom as flourishing within communal life, is a world away from the atomised and content-less self of classical liberal doctrine, and the neoliberal political-economic movement that derives from it. Part of Tony Abbott's success in the 2013 election was because he feinted towards that doctrinal ideal, and made an explicit compact with the voter that he would maintain the social policies that expressed such notions of collectivity – indeed, that he would execute them better than the chaotic Labor Party. Many of Abbott's difficulties in the first half of 2014 arose not only because he lied about his intentions, but because this lie embodied an attack on the very foundations of our collective life, as expressed in Medicare and other measures.

Just in case anyone missed the connection, Palmer has made a fetish of his obsession with JFK and the Kennedy clan, making an enormous donation to the John F. Kennedy Library Foundation, being appointed to its board and proudly photographed with Ted Kennedy, the bête-noire liberal for American conservatives. When Clive Palmer talks in his goofy hippy way about love and love revolutions, he's channelling an older sense of this, an idea of *agape*.

By now I can hear the guffawing, but a moment's honest consideration will bear out the case. Palmer has been completely consistent in doing what he said he'd do – vote to abolish the carbon and mining taxes – and completely in accord with his stated beliefs in developing a set of policies in response to the surprise budget. For six months he has said he and his party would not agree to the Medicare co-payment, the harsh new arrangements for unemployed youth, an increase in university fees or "assets recycling," and he hasn't. Much of what he was willing to compromise on with the government involved issues and policies peripheral to his philosophy. His rapid deal-making, a legacy of his real-estate and mining-lease years and his ability to package and repackage sets of options at a rapid pace seemed to bamboozle people, to convince them that anything was up for grabs. Yet this was nothing more than the horse-trading that is a necessary part of politics everywhere else, but that has been lessened by the lock-step nature of the Australian party system. One layer down is a set of core values, which are close to the centre of Australian politics.

Whether Palmer advances those values because he genuinely thinks about the single mum who wouldn't be able to take her kids to the doctor, and feels that we have a social obligation to her, or whether he imagines himself on the prow of a boat with cheering crowds garlanding him with flowers, as said single mum kisses him chastely and says, "Thank you for saving my baby's life," or some point in between the two, is of little moment. To ask what it is that a political figure believes him or herself to be is not to take that belief as true, or even seriously felt. But it is to presume that an idea about past formation will be a useful predictor of future action.

In the first half of the year we saw Tony Abbott treated with deference to his values and beliefs, as his chaotic and lying government slid from one side of the ring to the other, while Clive Palmer, ploughing a steady course on a range of key issues, was treated as the inconstant one. No wonder no one could tell what he was going to do next – they weren't even bothering to look at where he had come from. As Abbott moved out of the centre-right ground he had claimed in the election campaign, and Labor – infested with free-marketeers who would love the Coalition to introduce co-payments, higher university fees and welfare tightening so that they can continue them in a "progressive" fashion – refused to move into it, Palmer claimed it by default.

Doubtless it would be possible to over-interpret the man, but since there has been so little interpretation of him to date, the danger is slight. What would be an error, however, would be to seek to find in Palmer's life the key to his current hold on the political process. That hold came about not from any internal drive, but from external processes. Clive is not a cause of our current fractured politics: he is one of its most spectacular effects.

The South African people went to the polls, as a whole people, for the first time in 1994. With a vote of 63 per cent to 20 per cent for the nearest rival, they elected Nelson Mandela as their president. In 2002 the people of the new nation of East Timor went to the polls and elected Xanana Gusmão as their president by a margin of 83 per cent to 17 per cent. That's what you call a landslide, and a mandate for your program. In Australia, our greatest electoral triumphs have been of a rather different order: 56 to 44 per cent, and 55 to 45 per cent in the "landslides" against Labor in 1966 and 1975. In recent years, as political division has narrowed compared to the battle between capitalism and socialism of decades past, so too have the results. In 2013, winning 53 per cent of the two-party-preferred vote, Tony Abbott's Coalition team declared a "landslide," a designation much of the press gallery were happy to repeat unexamined, and to thus frame the subject for the general public. On the basis of that assertion, Tony Abbott claimed a mandate of such sweeping authority that MPs and senators who had been elected on an opposing program should put it aside and vote as one with the new government. It was rhetoric, of course, but its plausibility was based on the idea that a 53 to 47 vote constituted some expression of general will.

That is obvious nonsense, but over the years the conflation of an electoral victory with a change in the national mood has become so all-encompassing as to go almost unquestioned. A 53 to 47 result, put at the level of a tennis-club committee election, is an 11 to 9 result. Most people, in their everyday life, would recognise that as a close result. When translated to a national level, assisted by the "telescoping" effect translating a small majority of votes into a large majority of seats, it becomes wreathed in myth.

The same goes for our notions of popular movements and populism. Instead of uprisings, we have enthusiasms that surge for a while, transmit some of their ideas to established political organisations, and then dissipate. In 1996, Pauline Hanson, having been disendorsed by the Liberal

Party late in the election campaign, but remaining on the ballot, gained a 21 per cent swing and won the seat. Soon after, and with talk of a nascent political movement, a Roy Morgan Gallup poll indicated a party led by her would garner an 18 per cent primary vote. That was the closest anyone came to a populist groundswell – but, as we have seen, subsequent successes were fleeting, and the movement soon collapsed.

Compared to this, the idea that Palmer represents some sort of populist insurgency, or even a program for such, is ludicrous. Populisms of left and right, as movements within modernity – an era characterised by drawing the populace into ever more abstract systems of power – always hark back to the concrete and particular. The turmoil of the nineteenth century created modern anti-Semitism; the global mobilisations of imperialism brought forth the nativist socialist movements, with their brotherhood of white men, that would give birth to labour parties; the dislocations of the Hawke–Keating restructuring created the context in which immigrants could be blamed for a world being disassembled. From the start, Palmer's arguments – that boat-borne refugees should be treated more humanely and have other options made available to them, for example, and that running moderate deficits was no great problem – cut against the grain of populism. Nor did he, with any enthusiasm, marshal the angry resistance of "anti-politics" that others had tapped into (such as One Nation activists, in their dying days, who ran a "put the sitting member last" campaign), instead confining himself to a steady hum of remarks about how the old parties had failed and he was bringing about a love revolution.

By relentless advertising, he grabbed a large section of the Queensland electorate that Bob Katter had already detached from the major parties, and gained a boost from the high profile and respect that attached to his candidate there, Glenn Lazarus. In Tasmania, his cash injection allowed Jacqui Lambie to double a base 2 per cent, and paid for the expertise to concoct a preference deal that hoiked her up into parliament. In Western Australia, an election re-run allowed Palmer to pour as much money into the new election as all the other parties, major and minor, combined. The result was that his candidate got the nod, and the Australian Sports Party's Wayne Dropulich, previous winner of the micro-party slot, got dropuliched. Palmer himself won Fairfax with 26 per cent of the vote, and preferences – and a significant slice of his vote appears to be the result of a tactical decision by Labor voters eager to elevate him to second place. The same system that turns a small margin of victory into a significant majority of seats magnifies results like these into something that has the appearance of a movement. What would have occurred in the Senate had the PUP not existed is extremely difficult to calculate, but Stephen Luntz, a consultant psephologist to the Greens, has suggested that it is likely the Katter Party would have gained a seat in Queensland, as would the libertarian Sex Party in Tasmania, and the ALP's Louise Pratt in Western Australia. An absence of PUP votes in Victoria might have seen the Liberals' Helen Kroger elevated above Ricky Muir. Such a Senate would make the current chamber, in terms of stability and process, look like the Anglican general synod.

The PUP is a product of this system, of an interlocking set of political institutions that projects results back to the public as the expression of a general will. More particularly, Palmer and the PUP are a product of the Senate system, and its successive and unreconciled transformations. Founded on a first-past-the-post basis, the Senate system was changed in the 1920s to block preferential voting – in which one selected six names from an undifferentiated single list – which delivered such lopsided majorities as to make the chamber a dead letter for two decades. Before the 1949 election, with Labor heading for likely defeat, Arthur Calwell convinced Ben Chifley to change it to the proportional representation system – a variant on Tasmania's Hare-Clark system – as a way of hedging bets. This transformation created a working upper house – a genuine house of review, selected in a different manner to the lower house, allowing people to split their vote, or, alternatively, to give resounding endorsement to one party – but that in turn created a new (albeit minor) problem, that the entire ballot had to be numbered from 1 to 50, or 75, or however many, in order to register a vote.

Complex and bizarre as it may have appeared to many, the system had one great advantage: people could see where their preferences were going. But it also generated a higher rate of error, and hence wasted votes, among voters with low levels of education and poor literacy. When the Labor strategist Mick Young proposed a reform allowing people to "vote the ticket," with a single number in an above-the-line box, it appeared to be nothing more than housekeeping, the necessary completion of the 1948 process. However, the move had an unintended consequence: it made possible the creation of political advantage through the use of complex mathematics. Dummy parties, split preference allocations, "jump" preferences (where the preference flow jumps from one party list to another) and more have become the arcane tools of Senate campaign strategy. The age of the "preference whisperer" had arrived.

Nevertheless, despite the potential to game the system that accompanied the 1984 "above the line" change, it took thirty years before it was fully exploited, with the arrival of the PUP and the micro-parties. Why was this? Not because no one had spotted it. Front parties and complex preference swaps had made their appearance everywhere, from council elections to the student unions, where most of today's political leaders cut their teeth, to the New South Wales upper-house "tablecloth" ballot paper of 1999, which became famous around the world for its excessive number of candidates, and which marked the beginning of this form of strategising. Why has it taken so long for the system to be taken advantage of, given that the possibility was there for nearly three decades?

That lag is in part due to the extraordinary stability of the Australian political system. For the first half of the twentieth century, Australian politics was enormously fissiparous, with parties breaking and recombining and reforming, propelled by real political divisions around both the economic question and the imperial one (as came out in the conscription debate in World War I). From 1944 it has been extremely stable, even with the Labor split of 1954. From that time, with only the occasional interruption, the Senate has been a three-party system (counting the Coalition as a single unit): the DLP was replaced by the Democrats, who were replaced by the Greens. That stability has less to do with the calm good sense of the Australian people than it does with the system's extraordinary capacity to reproduce itself. Our major political parties are embedded in the system by the unique Australian "triple-lock": compulsory voting, exhaustive preferential voting and public funding of political parties based on their vote received. Thus, in all but a few seats in the lower house, the voter is compelled to the polling station, and further compelled, should they want their vote to count, to select either Labor or the Coalition. That gives these parties extraordinary heft to build large primary votes, for which they are then rewarded with tens of millions of dollars of public funds, so that they can advertise their brand the next time round. In effect, these parties are quasi-state apparatuses, desperate to maintain that triple-lock. When the Maoist activist Albert Langer found a loophole in the system in the 1990s, which permitted one to end a formal preference vote with two equal last numbers (that is, 1, 2, 3, 4, 4), thus nullifying the major parties, parliament passed a law explicitly banning the advocacy of such a tactic. When Langer breached an injunction barring him from advocating this type of vote, he gained a three-week jail term and status as an Amnesty prisoner of conscience.

This triple-lock in the lower house has, until recently, given the major parties the implied dominance necessary to getting large numbers from their lists elected to the Senate. The third parties have been smoothly integrated into the process, the DLP as Coalition supporters, and the Democrats and Greens tending towards Labor. Though Australian society has changed substantially in those seventy years, the system has had the capacity to absorb it. From the 1980s onwards, expansion of education created a growing class of knowledge/culture/policy producers. Previously attached to the left of Labor or to groups such as the Australia Party, they took first the Democrats and then the Greens as their natural home – to the point that the latter party now stands as their class representative.

The Greens party, too, benefits from the triple-lock system, and can reproduce itself over many election cycles by judicious preference swaps and smart allocation of resources – thus its 2013 dip to an 8.6 per cent primary vote saw it lose no Senate positions. The mainstream press's incessant deathwatch over the Greens ignores both the solidity of their class base and the stabilising effect of public funding. "A flawed party, internally divided," notes Paul Kelly of the Greens in *Triumph and Demise*, predicting afresh their imminent extinction. Quite aside from global cultural-political shifts, the triple-lock ensures that the Greens will be around a long time after Paul Kelly (not to mention the rest of us) has quit the field.

To repeat: that the Senate election of 2013 became a crapshoot is not the surprise – the surprise is that it took so long for someone to exploit the masked preferencing process that had been implanted in the system in 1984. That it did finally occur was due to a degree of political decomposition, largely on the right. Some on the left had considered, and decided against, running a slate of front parties, principally because such parties would draw support away from the Greens without necessarily coming back to them with additional votes, but also because progressive voters are more reflective and less easily manipulated.

The contemporary right is the home of the mythical, the nostalgic and the delusional, and a disproportionate number of its base are "low information" voters, while the ranks of its leadership are plagued with psychological instability (though the right does not have a monopoly on either). This is a habitat in which front and micro-parties can thrive. Nearly two decades after One Nation, with the multiculturalisation of Australia much further advanced and rural areas feeling yet more disconsolate at the withdrawal of subsidies, elements of the right were beginning to break away from the larger political formation. Katter's Australia Party had started the process at the federal level, and this was joined by the "federalisation" of a New South Wales process, the proliferation of shooters and outdoor recreation parties and tiny ultra-Christian groups, all defining themselves as "anti-elitist" representatives of ordinary Aussies, though usually established and run by sharp operators. Many of the people who would vote for these parties had genuine grievances, living in a society that has laid waste to areas of rural and working-class life without offering any sort of transition. Others were doing quite well, but lived in an intellectual climate framed by the Murdoch tabloid press and tabloid TV – populist "anti-elitism" produced in industrial quantities by university-educated, elitist journalists claiming to represent the unrepresented.

That these new groups began to emerge at a federal level and become autonomous players at a time when Tony Abbott, from the cultural right, took the leadership of the Liberal Party is only an apparent paradox. Abbott's victory was itself a sign of the fragmentation of the right, albeit one occurring within his party, because its right wing would not consent to a centrist candidate with (it was thought at the time) a greater chance of victory than Abbott. Once Abbott became prime minister, figures to the right of his right-centre position, such as Kevin Andrews and senators Cory Bernardi and Eric Abetz, began to run on a ticket of Christian right-wing cultural politics.

It was into this world, in the months before the election, that Clive Palmer injected his own brand of micro-politics. His determination to abolish the carbon tax undoubtedly attracted a section of the vote of the fragmented right – who were in for a surprise – but much of the additional support he gained was a case of pure projection onto a candidate who made himself omnipresent through big spending. To the fragmentation of the Australian political system he brought another element: plutocracy.

Clive Palmer is not the first Australian multi-millionaire to become a politician. Indeed, one of his United Australia Party antecedents was "Red" Ted Theodore, who became rich Ted Theodore, owner of the *Australian Woman's Weekly*. Clive's not even the only Australian multi-millionaire in the current parliament. Somehow, in all the kerfuffle about Palmer's entry into the hallowed House, the fact that the current Treasurer was worth something north of $10 million, and the Communications Minister had made a fortune in, erm, communications, was overlooked. But Palmer was the first to adopt a practice that has become increasingly common in the US, that of rich people simply buying their way into power, rather than wielding influence through bought-and-paid-for politicians. For every high-profile example of this – such as Michael Bloomberg, the business-TV billionaire who spent US$73 million winning the mayoralty of New York – there are numerous congressmen and women who have acted as autonomous players, in the merest cloak of party affiliation, and bought their way to Washington. (There have also been spectacular failures, such as Linda McMahon, the World Wrestling Entertainment entrepreneur who spent up to US$80 million trying to win a Senate seat from the right in Connecticut.)

The rise of American plutocracy is a product of the massive shift of money from wages to profits that has occurred in the US in the past thirty-five years, and of a revived and simplistic ideology of wealth as the product of individual initiative and personal virtue amid universal opportunity. But it could only have occurred because a countervailing power – that of organised labour, which underpinned the Democratic Party – had been so thoroughly undermined by aggressively pursued neoliberal policies that there was now no barrier to the mega-rich fusing financial and political power with apparent impunity. Once the process began, about a decade ago, it gathered pace, and occurred on both sides of the political divide. In Washington state, where this essay is being completed, not one of ten congressional districts (seats) is genuinely competitive, due to deals between the major parties. The only one that might have been was bought out of contention by the Democratic candidate, a Microsoft options millionaire. Dozens of Congressional races are now subject to this process, with more on the way.

Plutocracy never really took off in Australia. Lang Hancock had plenty of opinions, but he never started a party. John Singleton did, the so-called Workers' Party of the 1970s, an early entrant into anti-elitism by the elite, but it went nowhere. A suspicion of great wealth, rather than celebration of it, formed a stronger barrier to entry than existed in the US. It was all the more formidable, given that the Australian system has much lower barriers to entry. Clive Palmer appears to have bought himself a crucial role in the next three years of Australian politics for twelve million bucks, loose change for any number of multi-millionaires and billionaires on the Australian scene (including those who, unfashionably, have the cash ready to hand). He's the first to do so. Will he be the last?

Who is Clive Palmer? What is the meaning of him? Clive Palmer is the man at the centre of a perfect storm for Australian democracy in its actually existing form. He's a captain steering his vessel artfully in the whirlpool. He is a foolish passionate man, who has that endowment of the very rich, an erasure of the line between fantasy and reality, come along at a time when Australian political institutions had become sufficiently disarticulated to let him in with ease. Most people, especially those in the media, have become convinced that he is a man of no fixed character or beliefs, who rose to power through a rational political process. The reverse is the case. Palmer is a man with a coherent set of beliefs who is nevertheless a random product of an electoral process acquired in a fit of absent-mindedness.

That it was Clive F. Palmer, rather than Frank Lowy, Gina Rinehart or James Packer, who led the charge of the very rich into the realm of public institutional power was no accident: no one who has acquired or inherited and then consolidated money and power in a serious and focused manner – no one who has never wanted to be anything other than rich and powerful – would be so attracted to the exhibitionism and clowning that small-party politics requires. Palmer's will to take federal power has its obvious strategic and immediate interests, but it also offered itself to the globetrotting child-traveller, Gold Coast groover, poetaster and sometime steamboat captain as a stage for the performance of his many fantasies. That some of those fantasies coincide with a genuine public good – history may well record that it was Clive Palmer who saw off attacks on the universality of Medicare and unemployment benefits, and the full marketisation of higher education – is to our benefit, but it may well have been otherwise, and it was not the whole point of the exercise. Most very rich men are driven by a desire that stands outside of them, their rosebud, but Clive – well, Clive has so many rosebuds, he could make a wreath of them to send to his own funeral. Raised on ocean liners, he has been drawn back to boats and the water again and again, culminating in his announcement that he would be rebuilding the *Titanic*, effectively raising his boat-borne past from its watery depths, by replicating it. Fathered by a man who used a vast amount of radio equipment to survey the world, and had a mysterious and unexplained sojourn in China, he debugs his offices and does complex deals with China, all the while convinced that they have him under observation. A natural-born wheeler-dealer, he announced at an early age that he would follow the path of establishment propriety and become a lawyer, as per his mother's wishes. That commitment set up a war within him that lasted several years, until, in his early twenties, he was rescued by the necessity of making a living to become who he was always going to be: a salesman. Along the way, the boy who roamed the Gold Coast in its '60s heyday reassembled the playground atmosphere at a top resort in Coolum, and moved into his dinosaur principality, before honouring his mother's wishes and becoming not a lawyer, but a lawmaker.

We used to have a saying, in the trenches of cultural studies in the 1980s, that had Madonna not existed, it would have been necessary to invent her. Clive Palmer is of that line, but for trainee psychoanalysts. As far as desire, fulfilment and repression goes, it's all there where you can see it. But to say that his passions cross the line back and forth between fantasy and reality is not to discount either self-interest or cool-headed politics. It is to say that these things do not always come in neat packages. Palmer's invocation of a centrist politics with strong roots in Australian political tradition came at a time when there was mass opposition to the budget that was attacking such measures, but an inability by Labor to give an overarching moral account of why such a budget was wrong. Clive Palmer could, but what he couldn't do was switch out of the clownish mode that he had used to gain publicity during and after the 2013 election. That failure to project a more consistent and reasoned political style may have cost him his best chance to convert his freak win at the craps table of Australian democracy into a broader political movement.

OF DINOSAURS AND DEMOCRACY

People get angry at Clive Palmer. They get angry at him for his mercurial nature, for his half-arsed manoeuvres, for his obvious pursuit of vendettas, and for his ridiculous attempts to pretend that none of his politics has anything to do with his personal interests. But it is not Clive Palmer per se that is the source of this merry dance we have been on in the past six months. It is our current political arrangements, which are facing, if not a crisis of legitimacy, then something of a challenge.

Palmer's victory with his PUPs has focused attention on the Senate, but the disjuncture is more general. The single-member electorate system of our lower house is constituted on the nineteenth-century fiction that 150 duly elected people come to parliament after each election, and of their own free will and conscience constitute a government. Narrow victories telescope into substantial majorities, for parties that have been pre-constituted and whose members are interchangeable. When something actually happens which lives up to the pre-party notion of representative democracy – as in 2010, when five independent and small-party MPs were charged with choosing the government – everyone acted as if the place had suddenly become Mogadishu. When Tony Windsor and Rob Oakeshott exercised the Burkean privilege of voting on their conscience and best intelligence – having met with Tony Abbott, they decided that their electorates and the nation would do better under Julia Gillard – they were practically tarred and feathered in the main square.

Twice in one recent decade – 1990 and 1998 – the party that won a majority of the overall vote was denied a majority of the seats. In 1998 this was particularly disjunctive, with Kim Beazley winning 51 per cent of the vote, but only sixty-seven of 148 seats, with the Coalition taking eighty seats with 49 per cent of the vote. Had the Australian Electoral Commission happened to have chosen a different redistribution, our history would be different. Beazley would have been prime minister during 9/11, and, as an Americophile with a talent for the dramatic moment, he may well have risen to the occasion, and made Labor the party of national unity in the face of threat. Re-elected, he might well have been prevented by his party from committing to Iraq. How can any nation call itself a democracy and allow such a result to occur without deciding that some sort of reform is in order?

Of course, one of the reasons that people did not perceive 1998 as a crisis of legitimacy was because of the Senate itself – its checking role as second chamber. With the Democrats holding the balance of power and acting as a centrist party of review, everyone who was paying attention presumed nothing dramatic would happen. And nothing did, except comparatively – Meg Lees helped push through the GST, contrary to the clear preference of the voting majority. The move finished Lees, but since the GST had been proposed by Labor years earlier, it was hardly a matter of fundamental principle.

But there is another, and more important, reason why the now sclerotic apparatus of Australian government is not challenged, and that is because both sides of parliamentary politics, together with the media networks that attend them, have more in common with each other than they do with their supporters outside the charmed circle. Over the past two decades, the elite separation of political participants from the general public has become so marked as to constitute a historical breach. Before that breach, which took effect in the 1990s, there was significant traffic between the ranks of the general public and the political elite of the major parties, even if both were starting to fill up with political professionals. But in the past twenty years, the ranks of major-party parliamentary politics have started to close to those who have not dedicated their lives to it, from a very early age and overwhelmingly in the crucible of the universities. This is some-times referred to as the "political class," a phrase used by insider journal-ists trying to pretend they're not part of it. "Class" implies a group of some numerical size, which it isn't. It's a few thousand interconnected people, who draw others into their circle through a series of arcane political folk-ways and rituals, and thus replenish their number. It is, in other words, a political *caste*, sealed off from the general public, with the process of becoming a politician deliberately mystified to keep the amateurs out.

In such a set-up, the idea of challenging the system simply because you didn't win one election that you should have is laughable. You plan on being there for twenty years or so. That may be for the most principled of reasons or the most venal, or any point in between, but whatever the case, you know that the life of politics, for you, will be, in the last analysis, changing which side of the speaker's chair you're sitting on every six to ten years or so. Having committed to a life within this system, the last thing you want to is to start a process by which the general public questions it. The political caste also includes the vast majority of the press gallery, who live in a symbiotic relationship with the eternal parliamentary party, entombed together in the ghastly forbidden city of Parliament House – a building designed to make public access to parliament as difficult as possible, in a style that reminds one of Ceausescu's Bucharest "People's Palace" or all of Pyongyang – recycling minor gossip as news, and trading publicity for a drip-feed of information.

At its best, the Australian parliamentary press gallery applies a forensic attention to daily politics that is unparalleled in the English-speaking world. But overwhelmingly it has also absorbed the dominant ideology of eternal Australian politics, which is that politics is not politics – the clash of interests, ideas and belief systems – but policy. Policy, for the political-media caste, is Moses and the prophets. "Is it good policy?" they say in hushed tones. Their objection to the recent influx of new senators, like crashers at a suburban eighteenth birthday, is that they're not "good at policy." By policy they mean the steady and further neoliberalisation of economy, state and society. The political question then becomes one of quantity: how fast should this go, and how much in the way of "social market"-style checks and balances should be put in place for those blindsided by the process.

Across politicians and media, across the centre-left and right, there exists an undeclared cynicism about what this entails. The Australian public has never been sold on the neoliberal ideal that sits at the heart of policy idolatry – the political centre is a mix of left and right, of economic nationalism and social liberalism and conservatism, of sentimentalism and harshness. Occasionally, the political caste will do something that comes into contact with this bedrock reality – Howard's WorkChoices was the last example – and from the conflagration actual politics will occur. But it's something that they do their best to guard against.

How closed, sclerotic and self-reproducing is this version of democratic representation? Judge for yourself, by this paradox: the only way that its processes have come under question, and a conversation about democracy started, is by a passionate, clownish tycoon buying his way in, and a bunch of shadow-dwellers gaming the maths in order to slip their representatives onto the red benches beside him. Then, amazingly, we start to have a conversation about how the system can be "reformed" so that this can never happen again – the dreadful occurrence by which the Senate became a place where legislation was made on the floor of the chamber, in negotiations among individually elected senators! The horror! We heard about causes and issues – same-sex marriage, veterans' conditions, renewable energy, pokie machines – that hadn't been sanctioned by leaders of party business, to be led out by one or other interchangeable red-bench drone. Disaster! At times, it appeared as if much of the elite contempt for Palmer had nothing to do with the legitimate concerns about him – that he had bought his seats through blanket advertising, that he was advancing his own interests – but rather with a simple fact: by whatever means, for whatever reason, he has opened the door, and god knows who will rush in.

God knows indeed. Our system of federal power, designed for a monocultural federation of colonies with capital cities several days' travel from each other, has been transformed by a series of patches and improvisations that now constitute its core processes. Inductees to the political caste learn its arcane ways, and give their lives to it. The rest of the public – many of whom could no more formulate a plan of entry to politics than they could plot an ascent of K2 – look askance, increasingly conscious that they do not feel represented by their purported champions – in the way, for example, that Labor voters in an industrial capitalist society could feel represented by a patrician such as the late Gough Whitlam, even though they came from different worlds – and so they reject the opportunity to be patsies in an elite process. Thus, when polling comes along which suggests a legitimacy crisis – such as the recent Lowy Institute poll which suggested that 40 per cent of people don't believe democracy is the best system of government – we have a breakout of bogus soul-searching, and portentous nonsense about Grandad having fought for it, etc. Yet, of course, 40 per cent of people don't reject democracy. Where it can be really practised – in the body corporate committee, the kids' footy team, the tennis club – they practise it with sophistication and commitment. What the polls mean is that 40 per cent of people don't believe that our system of representation is either particularly effective or democratic, and they won't stand and smile and wave flags while their leaders pass by.

What, then, would precipitate a genuine crisis? Would it take a couple more people possessing eight-figure wealth deciding they'd quite like to buy a Senate seat, so that the issues of fluoridation, the Roswell incident and the decadence of jazz and race mixing can be raised in the upper house? Would it take a Senate ballot paper a metre long, scrolled out like a papyrus? Would it take a split vote/seat majority – of a 1998 magnitude – in the lower house, combined with a hung parliament? What if Tony Abbott receives a distinct majority of the vote in 2016, but Labor wins one more seat, and the government is decided, in Labor's favour, by an informal caucus of Adam Bandt, Andrew Wilkie and Clive Palmer, who can also guarantee the new government a working majority in the Senate? Would the Coalition accept that very, very possible scenario as legitimate? More to the point, would their supporters outside the political caste?

Maybe it will take an event of that magnitude to shake us from our complacency, our mistaking of torpor and disengagement for orderliness and legitimacy. If so, bring it on. But it would be better to start a conversation now, a real one, ranging across the country, about what sort of changes would make for a genuinely representative and more democratic system. That would involve discussion of multi-member electorates, voluntary voting, list systems, optional preferentiality, Senate thresholds, campaign spending, different models of public funding or its abolition altogether, the role of the governor-general, and beyond. Some of these measures face the near-impossible hurdle of a referendum, but many of them can be achieved by legislation. The most democratic way to re-ground Australian democracy would be for a series of such conversations to lead to a non-binding national plebiscite on proposals to reform our democracy, the results of which would guide subsequent bills in parliament. Any party that set itself against a manifest desire for change would expose itself as more committed to the system than to the popular will. Any attempt by big money to buy a result could be contested by the mass mobilisation of other groups. This is what we should have had as a genuine mark of the centenary of federation. But it is not too late now, and it would be better done in a spirit of cool intelligence and reflection than in the teeth of a crisis.

With, as we go to press, potential legal troubles mounting over Clive Palmer's use of CITIC payments for election campaign funding, and the irrepressible Jacqui Lambie channelling a hard-right politics alien to Palmer's centrism, PUP control of the Senate may come to an end sooner than most had supposed. That a would-be coal baron runs the crossbench's cross-bench – the three votes essential for the crossbench to go either way – is absurd, of course. But so too is having a Treasurer whose family fortune is constituted by his wife's skills as a banker, and whose family's future fortune will be considerably affected by the general decisions the Treasurer and his party make on taxes, interest rates, deductibility and the like. The party system masks this latter set of interests – Palmer's, at least, are right out there where we can see them. Palmer's immediate great and good service may be that his party has headed off attacks on the social system that, if successful, would open us up to full depredation on an American scale. But in the longer term we will only have come out of this period successfully if we are pointed towards an era when big beasts no longer, with such impunity, stalk the land.

1 November 2014

SOURCES

Despite repeated requests, it proved impossible to arrange an interview with Clive Palmer. Your correspondent approached Palmer's media advisor, Andrew Crook, his other media advisor, Phil Collins, and the great man himself on several occasions. Despite agreement in principle, all communication ceased.

Sean Parnell's page-turning biography of Clive came out before the 2013 election, and proved invaluable in gaining an insight into His Cliveness. The biographical sections of this essay draw extensively on that work.

James Dunk contributed additional research.

Knowing Clive, he will contradict everything asserted in this essay in the two weeks between its going to press and hitting the bookstands.

Megan Davis

I penned this response in the week that I, like many Aboriginal and Torres Strait Islander people, mourned the loss of the "Prime Minister for Indigenous Affairs", Gough Whitlam. When Noel Pearson delivered the Gough Whitlam Oration in 2013, he spoke of how the Old Man in his short time as prime minister had liberated Aboriginal people: "we were at last free from those discriminations that humiliated and degraded our people." Yet few Australians appreciate what that humiliation and degradation looks like, let alone feels like. *A Rightful Place* paints a compelling picture of this. It connects Australia's colonial history to the contemporary push for constitutional recognition and in doing so reveals why talk of symbolic recognition alone is repugnant to many Aboriginal people. *A Rightful Place* argues that to truly appreciate the recognition project and the exigency of substantive reform, one needs to understand the colonial project. One needs to be a student of Aboriginal history; Australian history.

Unbeknown to many Australians, from the late 1890s Aboriginal people were the subject of draconian protection – unfreedom – laws. Protection was required, in part, to prevent Aboriginal people from being indiscriminately murdered. It was the tail end of what we now know as Australia's first Great War: the frontier wars, as *A Rightful Place* describes to powerful effect: extermination as Scylla and protection as Charybdis. Yet the contemporary consensus of historians about the frontier wars has gained little traction in our polity. Why? As Pearson laments, "it is not the horrific scenes of mass murder that are most appalling here, it is the mundanity and casual parsimony of it all." That stinginess and casual indifference to the political economy of killing that built this great nation persists today.

A Rightful Place is an attempt to recalibrate the current approach to constitutional reform. Yet even before the Quarterly Essay went on sale, Pearson's potentially complementary proposal was dismissed as "grandstanding" and "unhelpful." Having served on the prime minister's expert panel on constitutional recognition alongside Pearson, I found this an exasperating reminder that although black leaders regularly chant "leaders are readers" to our young mob, Australia's political leaders are in fact, on the whole, not readers.

In 2012, too, the expert panel's report was criticised before the text was finalised. It was accused of over-reach for recommending a racial non-discrimination clause, although the historical and contemporary evidence of racial discrimination by the state is unassailable. Leaders remain attracted to preambular recognition despite the panel finding that constitutional thinking had moved on since the 1999 referendum and that stand-alone (second) preambles are too legally risky, apropos the unintended legal consequences of the 1967 referendum, which the current project seeks to correct.

Like Pearson, the expert panel took as its starting point colonial history. In *A Dumping Ground: A History of the Cherbourg Settlement*, the Queensland historian Thom Blake wrote:

> In the early months of 1901, as white Australians were undergoing their rite of passage into nationhood, another group of Australians were also participating in a rite of passage – but of a different kind. In the Burnett district of south-east Queensland, remnants of the Wakka Wakka tribe were being rounded up and dumped on a reserve on the banks of Barambah Creek. From camps on the fringes of towns and station properties, they had been forced onto an Aboriginal settlement established ostensibly for their care and protection. For the Wakka Wakka, their "rite of passage" was not into nationhood or independence but into institutionalisation and domination. The two rituals were diametrically opposed.

Blake clarifies the divergent paths of the Australian nation and Aboriginal people. He was writing a history of south-east Queensland's Cherbourg, set up by the Salvation Army member William Thompson in 1899, which in 1904 became a settlement under the *Aboriginals Protection Act*. My own mob was moved to Barambah reserve in the early 1900s from Warra. My grandfather and his siblings and many of my cousins grew up on Cherbourg.

The Cherbourg community has worked together to reclaim the old discarded Ration Shed – a symbol of the brutal regime of protection and unfreedom – where peas, porridge, flour, tea, sugar, rice and salt were rationed out to people on the mission. The old shed has been restored, together with the dormitories, and today is a thriving cultural precinct that includes an archive where people can research their family history. The Ration Shed's website proclaims that 121 Australian primary schools have visited the Ration Shed to learn about its history. It was on the verandah of this shed that the expert panel conducted its consultations.

Cherbourg's journey is an important one for the nation; it reveals – as Pearson, a "third-generation legatee of mission protection," suggests – that "the colonial enterprise does not tell a simple story." It is complex. In Cherbourg, they have reclaimed something that was brutal, even as the psychological and social manifestations of such unfreedom linger. This community has turned these dwellings into institutions of memory, survival and reconciliation: *Vergangenheitsbewältigung* – coming to terms with the past. The panel found moving examples of this all over Australia. *A Rightful Place* is a powerful argument for an appreciation of the good and bad in our history and that "complexity and nuance should not provide refuge from the truth that our nation's history includes times of unequivocal evil and times of redeeming goodness." History is inextricably linked to the recognition project. In the meantime these two groups remain unreconciled and disconnected despite, as Pearson powerfully implores us to see, indigenous culture including "the *Iliad* and *Odyssey* of Australia."

Where do we go from here? Is any form of "recognition" capable of overcoming the extreme economic and social disadvantage and unbelonging of our first peoples? If I return to Whitlam's incorporation into domestic law of the international norms of equality and racial non-discrimination, I note that this statute and this Old Man delivered more to Aboriginal people and Aboriginal rights than anything or anyone else. The contemporary unravelling of this is the subject of another Quarterly Essay, but Whitlam understood, thirty-five years before the United Nations General Assembly passed the Declaration on the Rights of Indigenous Peoples, that the right to self-determination was, for indigenous peoples, the path out of the devastation wrought by dispossession, decimation and protection.

Thomas Franck, in his watershed article "The Emerging Right to Democratic Governance," claimed self-determination is "the oldest democratic entitlement." Yet in modern Australia, the right to self-determination for indigenous peoples is conflated with sexual assault and corruption: an entirely fatuous and mischievous dismissal of a sophisticated political and legal concept. "ATSIC" – the Aboriginal and Torres Strait Islander Commission (1990–2005) – remains a dirty word: discussion of its flaws is well rehearsed, but its many virtues and substantive outcomes remain unstudied by academia and mistakenly conflated with separatism.

Writing in the *Australian*, Nicolas Rothwell noted that:

ATSIC was a peculiar beast: undoubtedly skewed towards south-eastern, "urban" Aboriginal interests, flawed and chaotic in its workings. Yet it was both a national indigenous voice and a conglomerate of strongly representative regional councils. Its members knew what services were needed, and delivered them. ATSIC built community houses in the interest of its own people, not outside contractors, and for a fraction of the costs incurred during the Intervention era's disastrous SIHIP program. The extensive bush infrastructure ATSIC left behind was well targeted and much remains to this day.

Yet on ABC TV's *Lateline*, when Noel Pearson announced his idea for an alternative approach, Tony Jones exclaimed: "But isn't this an ATSIC!" (*clutches pearls*), when in fact there is a crystallising sentiment that self-determination is a far sight better as a model than the ad-hoc, hodge-podge, top-down, paternalistic approach we have today, sustained by a vacuous faux-bipartisanship, as if our mob is undeserving of a contest of ideas when it comes to public policy.

There is in this current recognition project, as Rothwell rightly identifies, an "urgent desire of the political class for a single answer to the indigenous question … Causes like reconciliation, and its great successor, recognition, have an immediate appeal because they have universal application and promise a new landscape." The most deficient exhortation is that the cause of recognition is "special" and above politics. Actually it is not. It is complicated and it hurts your head. And globally it is an unremarkable exercise for any state to undertake. Yet it is the desire for a quick fix that is driving current momentum; and it is the urge to resist the quick fix that informs *A Rightful Place*.

One symptom of the quick fix has been the debate on symbolism versus substance: witness the exasperation of the political class at the prospect of a referendum being bogged down in issues of "wording." The esteemed journalist Michelle Grattan, one of the few apprised of the detail, observed in the *Conversation* that "for advocates of wide wording – surely it would be better to keep it narrower than have nothing at all? … Remember the apology." Grattan may as well be talking directly to the indigenous nations of this country, because it is we who are driving the preference for wide wording (substance) over narrow wording (symbolism). But if the injunction to "remember the apology" – a common refrain of advocates of symbolism – is aimed at the Aboriginal and Torres Strait Islander community, the response will not be gushing. A cursory glance at any Aboriginal newspaper since the apology would reveal huge reverence for the act, the day and the prime minister who delivered it, but an equal resentment at the lack of compensation. To not know that is to not know indigenous Australia. We know symbolism because that's what we usually get.

Another component of the quick fix is the suggestion that you don't need the votes of Aboriginal and Torres Strait Islander peoples to get this referendum across the line: a crude and repugnant constitutional calculation that requires no further elaboration.

A third manifestation of the quick-fix approach is the creeping cult of positivity that is descending upon any public discussion of indigenous issues. The mantra goes something like this: "only focus on the positive, only focus on the success stories." When beyondblue recently ran television advertisements identifying racial discrimination as a risk factor in anxiety and depression, there was a public backlash because it was considered to be negative and racist towards white people. "Why be so negative! Why focus on the bad things?" roared Twitter. The cult of positivity threatens this project because it disavows the humanity of the subject of recognition by preventing a conversation about what *A Rightful Place* is trying to put front and centre: "anonymous, extrajudicial, unreported, mundane."

Which brings me to the substance of the alternative approach contemplated in *A Rightful Place*. As Pearson makes clear, Aboriginal and Torres Strait Islander peoples approach the recognition project with history and questions of truth and justice in mind; this explains why sovereignty and a treaty are prominent features of discussion, however irritating this may be to the Australian polity. On the other hand, the Australian polity makes a political calculation based on the fact that only 8 out of 44 referendums have been successful since 1901, all under conservative governments. Therefore 8/44 × bipartisan support = minimalism; hence, surely it would be better to keep it narrow than have nothing at all? These are two very different starting points. One asks: what is just in the historical trajectory of invasion/settlement? The other: what is the compromise in the forty-fourth parliament?

The question of consent remains central to *A Rightful Place*, as Pearson contemplates the five permutations of the historical problem. When we went to Aboriginal communities during the expert panel consultations, most of us were struck by how alive and present this very complex question of sovereignty and a post-colonial settlement was. It was also clear to the panel that one of the reasons for the current movement towards recognition was not a burning desire to be recognised by Australia – a state-conceived project salvaged from the ashes of the failed 1999 referendum and arguably already achieved in 1967 – but to ameliorate the unintended (or intended) consequences of the drafting of the 1967 amendment. A corollary to the adverse use of the races power by the federal parliament is the suspension of the *Racial Discrimination Act 1975* on matters of importance to indigenous peoples, foremost among these land, heritage and culture.

Communities had vivid memories of *Wik* and *Kartinyeri* and the suspension of the *Racial Discrimination Act*, although they attract little media attention. Leaders still smarted that the *Wik* amendments had no input from Aboriginal people in the end. As Mick Dodson commented at the time, "What I see now is the spectacle of two white men – John Howard and [Senator] Brian Harradine – discussing our native title while we're not even in the room. How symbolically colonialist is that?" When ATSIC was abolished and a journalist asked Minister Vanstone what indigenous peoples would do now for representation, she replied that they had the ballot box. Not much comfort for 3 per cent of 22 million people. People still say they have no voice, no representation.

Here there is one problem – that of the elephant and the mouse – and two possible and equally valid solutions: one legal and one political. The recommendation for section 116A – a broad prohibition of racial discrimination – is a legal solution. It is aimed at disciplining the federal parliament. The second one, as implied in *A Rightful Place*, is a political solution not captive to short-term politics. *A Rightful Place* was unfairly portrayed by some as adversarial to the expert panel. It is not. There has not been any real debate on the section 116A proposal. Instead there is an oft-repeated, rarely questioned claim: conservatives won't accept it. They are not asked to come out and explain why. Even the interim report of the Joint Parliamentary Committee failed to give a plausible explanation for why it is problematic. We hear only vague mutterings about judicial activism and unelected judges. Is this a tacit admission by the political elite that changes to the constitution are for conservatives alone and that the people are a rubber stamp?

Yet the intuitive response of the people in 2011, at the end of the expert panel process, was – without prompting – 80 per cent in favour of a national commitment to racial non-discrimination: the only truly popular option of ours. Is this Australia, that 80 per cent? We may never know. The bottom line is this: the *Racial Discrimination Act* already has quasi-constitutional status and binds the states and territories. Section 116A aimed to bind the federal parliament. People quite like that.

On the other hand, as *A Rightful Place* pointed out, this runs counter to the Diceyan devotion to parliamentary sovereignty that dominates our political elite: that our parliamentarians can be trusted to do the right thing by the people and that the power of our parliament, unlike most in the world, should be completely untrammelled. Moreover, elected politicians should have the final say on the limits of their own power. Unsurprisingly, in our consultations, we found few Aboriginal people who subscribe to that Diceyan dogma. When we made the frank admission to them that a court applying section 116A is likely to defer to parliament, which could result in discriminatory legislation being enacted against the wishes of a community, they still had more faith in High Court than parliament: because it is expert, independent, unelected.

It seemed people felt the presence of section 116A might create a pause; an institutional tension or brake; a requirement to take time and consult; a requirement to go on country and talk to people before doing. That institutional pause is missing from our current political arrangements, at least when it comes to 3 per cent of the people. There is no compulsion for parliament to consult or take into account the views of the Aboriginal and Torres Strait Islander communities on any legislation or policy. The most uncomfortable flash-points in Australian history, when discriminatory legislation has been passed, have occurred without much media or popular attention.

A Rightful Place issues a challenge to conservatives who do not want their constitution encumbered by a right: you can't just be spoilers. What is the alternative to addressing the problem of the elephant and the mouse? In most comparable states there were treaties, and therefore indigenous peoples gained some form of "public" legitimacy from the outset. As we know, in Australia no such treaties were entered into. Instead, after *Mabo* we have this uncomfortable settled/conquered story, arrived at through litigation, which retrofitted invasion with a well-established land-tenure system. *A Rightful Place* suggests an alternative that seeks to preserve parliamentary sovereignty while providing the mouse with a place within the current political arrangements.

How have other jurisdictions dealt with the elephant and the mouse conundrum? They have reserve seats or designated parliamentary seats, indigenous parliaments, constitutionally entrenched rights, treaties made long after colonisation (post-colonial treaty-making) and other constructive arrangements. In my role in the United Nations Permanent Forum on Indigenous Issues, I am always struck by the creative ways in which almost all nation-states with indigenous populations have accommodated their voices in domestic political arrangements. It is the subject of much literature. As Pearson suggests, it is domestic political arrangements that accommodate indigenous peoples' voices and give full expression to the right to self-determination. If you perused some of this literature, you would see that self-determination is no symbolic, wishy-washy idea. It is about giving people control over their lives. It is not viewed as separatism, but as a way of enhancing democracy.

Pearson's alternative proposal is strategic too, because at the very moment they – the Joint Parliamentary Committee or the government – formally abandon section 116A, they will have a fight on their hands. Deleting the word "race" is simply preserving the status quo, maintaining the structural disadvantage. And the option proposed by the Joint Parliamentary Committee for a qualified race power (but not so as to discriminate adversely against Aboriginal or Torres Strait Islander peoples) is a poor trade-off for section 116A's broad prohibition. Pearson's catapult approach is not to wait for committees or leadership or a lacklustre national debate that waxes and wanes. Rather, he has offered up a still-to-be-debated alternative. He hasn't rejected racial non-discrimination. He has resigned himself to the fact that conservatives won't give an inch. No rights, right!

At the same time as we have seen resistance to the recognition project from conservatives, there has been a less publicised, yet surging resistance from our own mob – and it is not just about sovereignty and treaties. There are competing narratives that make the recognition task difficult: the right to bigotry, "unsettled or scarcely settled," severe funding cuts under the federal budget, especially in the justice sector (we are 3 per cent of the population but 27 per cent of the prison population), and the fact we are going backwards on some indicators in closing the gap. People have no voice.

The transcripts of the Joint Select Committee from public consultations in places such as Halls Creek, Broome and Fitzroy Crossing are solid evidence of this and well worth reading. People wanted to talk about the Commonwealth budget cuts, the impact of which were acutely felt in the Aboriginal and Torres Strait Islander communities, and spoke of insecurity, discontinuity, lack of autonomy and uncertain futures. In some locations, it seems, they wanted to talk about everything but recognition. It is apparent that in communities struggling to survive, recognition of recognition is low. The government-funded campaign Recognise has an unenviable task; it has no model, only a feeling. Through no fault of its own, Recognise has raised the suspicion of mob who dismiss such vagueness as "poetry," code for symbolism or the minimalist approach of deleting the word "race" without any regard for institutional racism: a disingenuous act of recognition by a nation of a community lagging behind its affluent counterparts.

A Rightful Place is a corrective to the path we are moving further down, the path of unfreedom. As Amartya Sen has argued, "development consists of the removal of various types of unfreedoms that leave people with little choice and little opportunity of exercising their reasoned agency." Rothwell similarly asks: "Do you, in fact, empower people by giving them the reins, and asking them to have a hand in shaping their own fate?" Will this constitutional recognition project bring a change in direction back to self-determination? As Pearson states: "no discourse can lean one way for too long. No wind can blow from one direction without restraint." Can Pearson win over a rights-reluctant conservative polity to a political approach acceptable to both the elephant and the mouse: the mouse taking the reins? And in all of this, will Australia accept that one possible outcome is that Aboriginal and Torres Strait Islander peoples might politely decline the offer of recognition? There must be room for us at least to have our voice heard on that: thanks but no thanks. Or maybe they'll forge on ahead as a nation without us. They always have.

Megan Davis

Rachel Perkins

Noel Pearson's hope, which I have come to share, is that "we stand on the cusp of bringing these three parts of our national story together – our ancient heritage, our British heritage and our multicultural triumph – with constitutional recognition of indigenous Australians."

I clearly remember when I came to terms with what that "ancient heritage" actually means. It was a winter day in Canberra. I was on my way to meet John Mulvaney, known as the father of Australian archology. He has deciphered the human life of our country. He has charted the great movements of change through two ice ages, as well as the small details of life, by sifting the evidence people left behind: the remains of kitchens and camp-sites, the use of fire and ochre, all layered in the earth over thousands of years. We were grappling with our documentary series *First Australians* and how to tell this epic story in just eight hours of television. If we were going to do the story justice, we needed his guidance.

No one in the scientific world now contests how very ancient is the occupation of Australia. It spans at least sixty thousand years – that's the conservative estimate. I asked Mulvaney how we might communicate this profound depth of time to our audience. An explanation of archeological methodology wasn't going to cut it on TV. His gentle words that day have stayed with me. He explained that the arrival of the First Fleet occurred *five* generations ago. He then explained that human occupation, before the First Fleet, traces back 2500 generations. Translating the concept into the lives of generations enabled me to begin to grasp the immeasurable human experience: the dreams, the love, the birth and death of these people, felt across the continent. About *a billion lives*, he estimated. That's a lot of life. I remember his eyes twinkling as they observed me grappling with the project to which he had given his life: understanding the depth of Australia's humanity.

First *Australians* ultimately began with his words and ended with the High Court's *Mabo* judgment acknowledging native title. The overwhelming response to the series, after it was broadcast on SBS, was, "Why weren't we told?" People felt denied. They were resentful about their lack of knowledge of the history of the country. From this experience I understood how fundamentally the institutions and the structures of our society have failed to provide our citizens with any understanding and ownership of their deep Australian heritage.

Mulvaney's great friend of equal brilliance was Dr Norman Tindale. Confounded by the ignorance of most Australians and their view that "Aborigines wandered around the land," he set out on an epic personal project to map the territories of the first Australians. I asked Mulvaney how Tindale could conceive of taking on a personal project of that scale off his own bat. He said, "You'd have to know the sort of man Tinny was to understand that." I wish I had. It took fifty years to complete.

I have a copy of the map, found by friends at a garage sale. It comes in four large scrolls, each showing a quarter of the continent. Together they take up an entire wall in my office. This was his statement to the world. People who visit our office are stopped in their tracks by the map. They are rendered speechless at the detail it reveals. It shows around 250 groups, each with its own language and land holdings. Visitors immediately respond by either finding their own ancestral tribe, or the tribe's territory in which they live. In that moment they step into Australia's deep past. They also see the present, the underbelly of our nation, with the very recent straight lines of our federated states drawn across its surface. This map is a revelation for people, which emphasises Noel's point that "there is no official recognition of the many tribal nations associated with particular territories."

It is often stated that we have longest continuing culture in the world, but what does that actually mean? It means this: we had an ocean surrounding us, and our distant position on the other side of the earth meant we were invaded later than everyone else. Our civilisation was not disrupted, so our culture was and is continuous. This means that in many parts of the country the very ancient rock art is still understood. Consider that for a moment. People here are still connected to a civilisation far more ancient than that of the Romans, Greeks and Egyptians, than that which produced a site such as Stonehenge in its antiquity. We still understand the rich stories and meaning behind these epic ancient masterpieces. The stories are still with us – mostly. The question is: do we care?

High on the cliffs at Bondi Beach there is a whale carved into the sandstone. There are about 2000 carvings like this, inscribed into the soft Sydney sandstone

– which makes the city one of the largest galleries in the world. I sometimes walk up there and pause beside the carving. It is positioned to give a magnificent view of the ocean from the south-east edge of Australia. This is the point from which the Gadigal people witnessed the twelve ships making their way northward to Warrang, now known as Sydney Harbour. I imagine them standing there looking out to sea. But turn your head, and you are visually assaulted by fluoro joggers hammering past. For me, this site sums up Australia's relationship to its national heritage. We have never paused in sufficient numbers for long enough to truly consider it. To wonder about the hands that created the whale, what it might have meant to those people – to begin to understand it and ultimately to make it our own. We are in the process of running past our Australian heritage in the pursuit of a fluoro future.

Recently the prime minister nominated the arrival of the First Fleet as the defining moment in Australian history. Not unexpectedly, he was widely criticised for ignoring the depth of prior human experience. But I agree with him. I think it is the most significant event, but not for the same reason. The arrival of the First Fleet meant the building of a new society much like that found in most Western capitalist states, one which now boasts twenty-three million people. But it has destroyed, in part, an incredibly distinct society created across the deep time that Mulvaney has revealed.

The tsunami of colonisation that followed the First Fleet crashed across the south of our continent and swept north for another hundred years. One measure of its impact is the decimation of Australian languages. Noel quotes Johann Gottfried Herder on the importance of language:

> Has a people … anything more dear than the language of their fathers? In it lives its entire wealth of thoughts about tradition, history, religion and principles of life, all its heart and soul. To take from such a people their language or debase it amounts to taking from them their only immortal property, which passes from parents to children.

We have lost more than half of our original Australian languages. People are working hard to revive them, but the situation is grim and accelerating. By 2050, only fifty of the 250 are expected to survive. Language is the net that catches the intangible cultural knowledge: the place names, spiritual beliefs, environmental knowledge and, of course, the songs which carry the dreamings – the stories of how the world was created.

In considering a place for Aboriginal and Torres Strait Islander people within the nation, Noel explores what colonisation meant for the Tasmanian Aboriginal people. They felt the full force of the tsunami. He eloquently pays respect to the old people of that community, who saw the cold reality of their fate squarely before them: to be removed from their lands and have their way of life denied them. In researching First Australians, I also traversed this history and that of many other communities in the south, where colonisation occurred earliest and in earnest. I searched for traces of their classical culture: songs, paintings, photographs, letters, anything we could find to fill out the story of their time. But as with the whale on the cliffs at Bondi, the detailed meaning has largely been lost.

Communities are rebuilding, and their hard work is testament to how they cherish their culture. Their land and waterways provide a foundation for the reclaiming of knowledge, and the tribal boundaries and identity remain strong. This is our great resilience, to hold our identity dear, despite all the forces of colonisation and society conspiring against us.

In Noel's 2009 Quarterly Essay, *Radical Hope: Education and Equality in Australia*, he asked another very direct and more personal question of us. I shuddered when I read it, wanting to avoid what was being asked of me.

> It is time to ask: are we Aborigines a serious people? Do we have serious leaders? Do we have the seriousness necessary to maintain the hard places we call home? Do we have the seriousness necessary to maintain our languages, tradition and knowledge?
> I strive to avoid wishful thinking but one can never be immune from it. The truth is I am prone to bouts of doubt and sadness around these questions. But I have hope.

After avoiding Noel's question for years, I decided to get serious. I and senior Arrernte ladies, along with the ethnomusicologist Myfany Turpin, are attempting to record our women's songs and the dreaming stories they carry.

Noel writes, "Australia does not have a comprehensive agenda for the recording, preservation, presentation and utilisation of the country's heritage ... Much of this knowledge will be lost if we do not grasp the importance and the urgency of this work." He describes the recording work we are doing in Arrernte country as "one example of the urgent work that needs to be done Before It's Too Late (BITL)." He goes on to lay out his aspirations for BITL Mark 3: a national project to record classical culture and revitalise existing cultural collections, with concerted public support.

Noel's notion of tethering cultural survival to constitutional reform is intriguing. When I grasped the potential of his idea, I realised it may be our best hope – in the short term – of attracting national interest on this issue. It lit a spark for me and gave me hope, for we have only to look back on our history to understand the trajectory we are on. The question is: will our people be able to put their differences aside and unite, as they did in 1967, towards this possibility?

Noel spoke bluntly but truthfully in his 2009 article "A People's Survival":

> Aboriginal Australians need to be brutally honest about the threatening demise of Aboriginal culture. We need to face the evidence and be less rhetorical. The cultural survival of Aboriginal Australian peoples does not hinge on declaratory assertions that "We have always been ...", that "We will always be ..."

Certainly, Noel has the seriousness required to push the case for recognition and a national indigenous cultural agenda. I intend to stand by him in that cause. I encourage others to do so, with us, BITL.

Rachel Perkins

Celeste Liddle

A Rightful Place focuses a great deal on arguments in support of the recognition of Aboriginal and Torres Strait Islander peoples in the Australian constitution, and particularly on persuading conservative opinion-holders. Pearson makes a number of salient points and his case for broad support is mostly eloquently put. As the question is whether a referendum on this issue can be successful, Pearson is correct to focus on the entire electorate, as a majority of voters in a majority of states will need to vote "yes" in order for the referendum to pass. In short, the essay gives a well-rounded perspective on the Aboriginal case for constitutional recognition.

However, while Pearson addresses the mainstream opposition, he does not discuss indigenous opposition to any degree. I don't feel this is a flaw in his work, as his position is clear: he supports constitutional recognition for Aboriginal and Torres Strait Islander peoples and wishes to bring voters from all sides on board to ensure the success of a referendum. I do, however, feel it is a major flaw in the dialogue around this issue that warrants further exploration. The "anti" stance has been dominated by conservative white men – including the constitutional conservatives Pearson mentions – while support for the move has been dominated by more moderate indigenous opinion-holders and government-funded campaigns. Whether indigenous people themselves wish to be recognised in the constitution should be at the heart of this discussion; otherwise, we run the risk of indigenous recognition being another merely symbolic gesture.

There is a long history of failed policy when it comes to Aboriginal and Torres Strait Islander affairs. We have had generations of "good intentions" (or so we're told when historical reflection occurs), yet our social markers suggest we are still the most disadvantaged people in this country. Additionally, we have heard so many grandiose statements, and seen so many broken promises, that many indigenous people tend to be quite cynical and discerning when presented with political pledges. A recent poignant reminder of the source of such cynicism was former prime minister Bob Hawke's address at the 2014 Garma Festival. During his speech Hawke confirmed that he supported constitutional reform. The fact that, as prime minister, he had promised a treaty only later to renege on this did not go unnoticed. If he had followed through on his 1988 promise made at Barunga, it is highly possible that we would not be having this conversation about reform now, or at the very least the framing would be quite different.

We also have a cynical view of moves perceived to be mainly symbolic. The 2008 apology to the stolen generations is an example of an act that some indigenous Australians see in this way. Many found Kevin Rudd's words healing and engaging, and the warmth with which he delivered them was welcome after years of Howard rule; however, the clear statement from opposition leader Brendan Nelson that "there is no compensation fund", a point which Rudd avoided completely in his speech but later confirmed, cast a nasty shadow over the event. What's more, there appears to be an understanding in the national electorate that the apology was "to Aboriginal people" rather than for the policies that led to the stolen generations. On its website, the Australian government fuels this misconception by labelling the event the "Apology to Australia's Indigenous Peoples." When we hear conservative media commentators capitalising on this by asking when indigenous people will ever be satisfied, it's not hard to see how such views gain traction in the broader population.

The Recognise campaign is itself a source of contention within the indigenous community. For every indigenous person who supports or is opposed to constitutional reform, there would probably be another two who are simply unsure. The Recognise campaign was developed to educate Australians on the benefits of recognition. It bills itself as a "grassroots campaign," yet it has been allocated $10 million in government funding over two years to deliver its message of reform – a message which is consistent with the current government policy platform. Its focus on advertising has become apparent, with corporate entities such as Qantas emblazoning aeroplanes with giant Recognise logos. Conversely, opposition movements have been reliant on social media to get their messages out and connect with like-minded community members. The opportunity for indigenous people of differing opinions to participate in a debate on an issue that is going to primarily affect their communities has simply not been provisioned for. From an indigenous perspective, there are serious questions about how democratic this process is. Dissenting views are only now gaining a slight amount of traction.

So what are these oppositional indigenous views? First, it is important to understand that rather than being homogenous, those opposed to constitutional recognition come from a vast variety of backgrounds. If I were to put them on a spectrum, I would place at one end the Black Nationalist movements and at the other holders of the view that recognition is an unnecessary distraction from tackling other, more life-changing, issues. I won't go into the latter view as it seems to be held by more conservative commentators and it is for them to highlight their arguments. Of the other anti-recognition views, though, some reinforce indigenous sovereignty and call for treaties, while others seek emancipation from the state entirely.

It is unsurprising that at this point in time we are seeing more tent embassies and more public acts reinforcing indigenous sovereignty than we have for years. Recently, four young Aboriginal activists re-entered the country using Aboriginal passports, causing some confusion customs. In 2013, the Murrawarri Republic undertook a secessionist movement and sent a declaration to the Queen, Prime Minister Julia Gillard and the United Nations. A First Nations Women's Ceremonial Walk for Freedom was recently organised. These are just a few examples. People making moves to emancipate themselves from the laws of this country are not going to have a great deal of interest in recognising the highest law that exists, the constitution, and are therefore not putting their faith in the idea that amending it will right wrongs done to indigenous people and lead to a more equitable society.

Noel Pearson discusses in great depth the concept of layered identities. I found this of particular interest, as it is partly the reason why I find myself on the oppositional side. I am Arrernte, but I also identify as a feminist and a trade unionist. Like Aboriginal people, women were excluded from the table when it came to the writing of Australia's constitution. This country still has a long way to go before it achieves gender equality. As a trade unionist, I support a hearty process of negotiation between parties wishing to work together to achieve outcomes. There has never been a negotiated agreement between First Peoples and the government in this country and I feel that it is integral to achieve this before we look at amending the constitution to include Aboriginal and Torres Strait Islander people. Pearson is absolutely correct when he highlights that treaties negotiated with other indigenous peoples in the world have rarely been honoured. Due to this fact, Australia has a wealth of knowledge globally on which to draw and improve. To me, the idea of simply being recognised is an act of unquestioning consent to this Australian authority and I'm really not of a mind to be a "blushing virgin" in this instance.

Pearson makes many solid arguments for his case, and it is clear that he is dedicated to a future of unity between Aboriginal and Torres Strait Islander people and the broader Australian population. The problem is that indigenous people themselves are not committed to this idea of "unity," nor are numbers of them convinced that it will bring anything of the sort. Despite the legal fiction of terra nullius apparently being a thing of the past, many people feel it still permeates society today, and therefore being written into a document which was based on the premise of terra nullius is not the answer. We owe it to ourselves and the experiences of our forebears to ensure that we tread lightly here, examine the question from all angles as indigenous peoples, and then engage the greater Australian public in these debates.

Celeste Liddle

John Hirst

Despair at Aboriginal affairs takes different forms. The philanthropist Andrew "Twiggy" Forrest wants to keep money out of Aboriginal hands. Aborigines would still receive welfare, which is what sustains most remote communities, but only as an entitlement to buy certain goods, which would not include grog, drugs and pornography. In *A Rightful Place*, Noel Pearson has joined other Aboriginal leaders in believing that changes to the constitution are a remedy for Aboriginal woes.

At first glance Forrest's proposal seems more likely to bring an immediate, beneficial result. If Aboriginal communities are destroying themselves with alcohol and drugs, let's prohibit access to these substances. Even if this were to succeed – and one can think of many ways the prohibition might be avoided – would it produce what people of goodwill want to see: Aboriginal people living well on their own lands? The ingredient that is missing to make healthy people and communities, and which a hundred programs and billions of dollars have not so far produced, is a sense of responsibility in individuals so that they would care for themselves, their children and their communities. Many years ago, W.E.H. Stanner identified a silent resistance to the invaders, which is still there despite all that has changed in public policy since. It is as if remote Aborigines are ready to risk their own destruction rather than be what we want them to be (which surely is no longer paternalistic: what we want must be what they want too; surely they want to "close the gap?").

Noel Pearson was the first Aboriginal leader to set aside all slogans and excuses and identify the missing ingredient. He has created new institutions in Cape York to encourage or even enforce a sense of responsibility. These have required changes to the law and large injections of government money. One of the many puzzling passages in this essay is Pearson's attempt to show that Aborigines are without influence in this polity.

There are mixed reports coming out of Cape York on the results of Pearson's initiative. I fear that he himself must have doubts because of his willingness now to reach for explanations and solutions which formerly he would not have countenanced. Previously, in *Up from the Mission*, he wrote: "why has a social breakdown accompanied this advancement in the formal rights of our people?" And in case you were ready with an answer about exclusion and exploitation, he added: "this social breakdown afflicts with equal vehemence those Aboriginal peoples who have never been dispossessed of their lands and who retain their classical traditions, cultures and languages." This was the preamble to the insistence that Aborigines had to stop blaming others and assume responsibility for themselves – and get off welfare. Now he argues that Aborigines have never had real liberty, that the collapse into welfare dependency was not an irresponsible choice because it was not a choice of a free people who could choose development over welfare. This overlooks that numerous schemes to run businesses on traditional lands have been tried and mostly failed; that where jobs are available in remote Australia it is often not the local Aborigines who take them; that where Aborigines have been paid royalties for mining on their lands the proceeds have usually not been well spent and everyone remains on welfare; and that Aborigines still control huge swathes of territory and large mineral deposits and can debate among themselves the terms for the development of these areas (another sign, by the way, that Aborigines are not marginal people in this polity).

Pearson can put very forcibly the case that real choices have been made and by people wanting, as is very human, incompatible things: "I want to maintain my traditional cultures, but I still want to have all the vices of the Europeans"; "I want passive welfare to enable us to maintain our traditional lifestyles."

These are Pearson's formulations, but he urges us to dismiss them in favour of a tortured argument about the amount of liberty and when choices are real choices. Of course choice will always be restricted by opportunity and capacity, but to argue that Aborigines have had no choice but to live on welfare is absurd. Many Aborigines do prefer welfare to what policy-makers want for them and have offered to them: regular work, money-making, kids in school.

According to Pearson, the diminution of Aboriginal liberty relates to their position in the constitution: both the failure to recognise their claim as indigenous owners and the classification of them as a race. Hence, their rescue will come with constitutional amendment. I admit I find it difficult to give a fuller account of an argument that I find totally unpersuasive.

The classification of Aborigines as a race in the constitution is very indirect. The constitution allows the Commonwealth to make laws for any race for whom it is deemed necessary to make special laws. Under this provision the Commonwealth gets its ability to pass laws on Aboriginal affairs. If this section is removed, some other provision will have to be made to allow the Commonwealth to legislate. There would not be a hundred Aborigines in the country who know they are classified as a race for this legislative purpose. If Pearson knew of this before, only recently has he become aware of its high significance, about which he writes with the dismay and passion of a convert. Pearson is confident that its removal would be much more than symbolic; it will lead to a psychological transformation in Aborigines, who will no longer be a race and so they will think of themselves and stand before us as a people with a distinct heritage, with their own cultures and languages, which is how they have seen themselves and been seen by others for the last forty years. Part of the case for removing "race" in the constitution is that it is a term that has been comprehensively excluded from all our other talk.

Pearson begins his essay with a poignant account of Galarrwuy Yunupingu fearing that his Yolngu world will disappear even though his people occupy their traditional lands. After all his pleas to politicians and their courting of him, nothing is any more secure, everything may be swallowed up by the whitefellas. His wish that his culture might continue is very different (as Pearson points out) from what Canberra thinks everyone is agreed on as Aboriginal policy: "closing the gap." Pearson's long excursus in this essay on the fate of the Aborigines in Tasmania is designed to remind us of the enormity of what we now face: the final elimination of an ancient culture.

Some proposals for constitutional recognition include respect for or maintenance of traditional cultures and languages. Yunupingu looks to the constitution to protect "our way of life in all its diversity." Pearson supports these proposals without offering details. The problems that would ensue from such provisions are immense – what is traditional culture? is all of it to be respected? who is to judge? – but no provision in constitution or law can limit the forces that are threatening the world of the Yolngu. Yunupingu wants whitefellas to conjure up something to stop his young people taking drugs, showing no respect for traditional culture and watching rubbish on screens! He has more chance of doing that than we have. Thinking that all those politicians could help him was a false move. He realises this himself in the essay from which Pearson quotes: he has to take responsibility.

I am in favour of recognising Aborigines in the constitution. I have suggested a form of words for the preamble in which this could be effectively and safely done:

And whereas the people of the Commonwealth acknowledge that all its lands were owned by the Aboriginal and Torres Strait Islander peoples who retain rights to them as set out by the High Court in its judgements in *Mabo* and *Wik*.

Pearson does not accept the significance of *Mabo*. He writes that there has been no settlement of the original act of aggression. Nothing now proposed in alteration of the constitution will be of more significance than *Mabo*, which declared that the Aboriginal people were the original owners of the country and were still the owners of so-called Crown land if they could show that their traditional ties to it still existed. Saying that nothing has in essence changed is a necessity for those who think they have at last found the formula that will bring success.

That is the role now cast for constitutional recognition. It has morphed into a new cause that will solve all that hasn't been solved so far and what in truth may be unsolvable. That will burden the constitution to no one's benefit except the lawyers. It is antipathetic to the Australian political tradition, which does not look to constitutional provisions to define the people or constrain policy. Aborigines are already part of polity and if they have programs that look like they will bring success, they will be listened to – as Pearson was. That does not await constitutional recognition. If Aboriginal communities are to revitalise themselves, it will not be done by seats in parliament or some national reference group to advise on Aboriginal legislation, other ideas that Pearson floats in this essay. If Galarrwuy Yunupingu asked for the control of social welfare payments and the Aboriginal budget for his territory, I would give it to him.

In parts of the essay, Noel Pearson shows those qualities that make him a gift not only to Aboriginal people but also to the nation at large. Of the historian Henry Reynolds, whom he does not spare from criticism, he writes: "He has been about finding grace for the nation by breaking the silence on Aboriginal history and all the time being faithful to Australia." These words could well be said of Pearson himself. But in my view the cause of constitutional recognition has taken him down a cul-de-sac.

John Hirst

Henry Reynolds

A Rightful Place is an admirable addition to the Pearson oeuvre – intellectually bracing and cogently argued. Peppered with apt references to and quotations from a wide assortment of authorities, from Johann Herder to T.S. Eliot and H.G. Wells, from Amartya Sen to Roger Scruton and Robert Hughes. Along the way we come across engaging glimpses of Noel's childhood and his community of Hopevale, just north of Cooktown. But the essay does not stray far from its charted course. It is a forensically powerful polemic about the future place of indigenous Australians in what he calls "a more complete Commonwealth." As the argument unfolds, Pearson makes many pertinent observations on the nature of democratic societies – and Australian political culture, in particular. There are allusions to the universal fate of cultural and ethnic minorities and their struggles for survival. *A Rightful Place* is a valuable addition to the nation's political literature.

But a polemical work does not stand alone. It cannot be detached from the cause in contention. It is judged and maintains its relevance only so long as the circumstances which called it into existence prevail. The final brief chapter, "Making Peace," brings the argument home to the "national challenge" of achieving a "yes" vote in a coming referendum on constitutional recognition for indigenous Australians. Noel has been intimately involved in the process and was a member of the panel that proposed to government a draft bill incorporating amendments to be put to the electorate.

The essay leaves behind a strong sense of dislocation, a mismatch between the powerful plea in the body of the work for a new relationship between indigenous and settler Australia and the extremely limited and cautious proposals to be incorporated in the referendum. There is more passion than ambition. There are reasons for this, of course. Noel and the other panel members were fully aware of the history of failed referendums and the need to have bipartisan support as well as a large majority of the electorate on side. And the difficulty of this task cannot be underestimated. But the panel limited its own task when it began by defining the four principles which would govern its deliberations. The first – to contribute to a more unified and reconciled nation – was the most important. As with the whole process of reconciliation, the hidden implication is that indigenous Australia has to do far more reconciling than the rest of us. And the reference to a unified nation is a give-away. It embodies the continuing Liberal Party commitment to assimilation. A straight line can be drawn here from the policies of Paul Hasluck in the '50s through Howard's One Nation to Abbott's Team Australia.

The proposals to strike out references to race in the constitution are timely and unlikely to be seriously challenged. But the two clauses relating to recognition do little more than state the obvious and uncontested. New section 127A will recognise indigenous languages as part of our national heritage but establish English as the national language. There is nothing here to prevent future governments from determining that English should override indigenous languages in education. New section 51A has a similar reference to the obvious, declaring that Australia was first occupied by Aboriginal and Torres Strait Islander peoples.

This brings us to the heart of the matter. "Occupy" is such a carefully chosen word, presumably devoid of legal purchase, purposely sidestepping the question of prior indigenous sovereignty. The panel was aware of this problem. Many submissions referred to the question. But concern about likely community reaction to any reference to either sovereignty or self-determination merged easily with the overarching conservatism of the panel itself. So a successful referendum would leave the fundamental questions untouched: were the indigenous nations sovereigns? If so, how and when did Britain acquire that sovereignty? Does any remnant of sovereignty reside in indigenous society?

Noel Pearson's powerful advocacy notwithstanding, Australia has regressed on indigenous matters – a generation ago the question of a treaty was seriously discussed, as was the status of traditional law. And this leaves us far behind comparable societies such as New Zealand, Canada, the United States and the Scandinavian countries. Noel argues that we cannot expect any more because, unlike the Maoris, indigenous Australians are only a very small minority. But this carefully avoids comparison with the much higher status of the Native Americans in North America and the Sami in Scandinavia.

The eloquence of *A Rightful Place* points in one direction; the political agenda directs us elsewhere.

Henry Reynolds

Peter Sutton

'My thoughts flash back to the warriors who fought the colonial
invasion ...'; 'I cannot take my mind off William Lanne ...'; 'I want
to re-remember what happened in [Tasmania] ...'; 'I indulge my
own nostalgia by sharing those things that possessed me as a boy
...'; '[the death of Truganini was in] the primary-school curricu-
lum of my childhood ...'

Noel Pearson's language in *A Rightful Place* reflects a new phase in his trek as an
intellectual and as a person. It is time now to think more on the past, and, also,
on what it is to be indigenous, on what it is to be an Australian, and on what it
is to be. Pearson's reform trajectory, one that began with the legal achievements
of land rights, and midway added an incandescent focus on the restoration of
social functionality to communities in deep trouble, has moved again. It is not
a shift from action to contemplation in any simple sense, but it is in some sense.
Noel's own mellowing struggle with the terms of belonging is projected here
onto the wider screen of the various peoples of the commonwealth. This wrestling all night is not in vain. It leads him to put the psyche back into what it is
to be a citizen, complementing what is so often a reduction of the political
personage to a rights-bearing participant in the economy.
    Noel writes in the essay of:

'existential angst', 'the great existential enigmas'; 'existential anxieties', 'psychological discomfort'; 'a legitimate anxiety'; 'the emotional convulsions of identification and memory'; 'the psychological
meaning of this historical legacy'; 'this historical and spiritual
turmoil'.

On this occasion:

> I am not now concerned with the legal question [of indigenous relationships with territory]. I am concerned with the metaphysical question: the *spiritual notion*.

This is why, in the essay, Noel is able to frame the constitutional issues other than by legal and political lineaments alone. I think this saves them from being less engaging, less interesting, less alive, than they will be if they remain forever in the secular combat zone of structure and rights. Here Noel walks gingerly the fulcrum of a seesaw. Tipping in one direction, one might suppose, are social unity and integration, which are matters of structure. Tipping in the other, perhaps, are past-based identities and cultural distinctions, which are much more matters of feeling and value. But it is too easy to consider the structural unity of the modern liberal nation-state as not being composed also of tradition, of the past, of feeling. And it is likewise too easy to consider the rootedness in the past of traditional identities as having a life apart from the superstructure of government, industry, education and the media. Once again, here, Noel is offering a radical centrism, one in which structure and peoplehood have to meet the elemental demands of the psyche for a home, a haven.

In other words, if the coming constitutional amendments do not nurture the soul, they will be as chaff. The next liberation in Noel's to-do list has to be "psychological." He does not say "emotional." This difference matters, as it is the psychology of the emotions surrounding identity and the post-colonial self as an embodiment of history that is his concern. It is about feeling but it is even more about a thinking awareness of feeling. This is the hope for those who endure troubled and anxious times about who or what they are. One thing they need to be relieved of is the notion of belonging to a native "race." The self, not just the constitution, and not just popular ideas of indigenous peoplehood, has to be de-racialised.

Reforms to the constitution, chief among which should be the removal of the notion of race, will be "not just a matter of symbolism. I think this will be a matter of psychology." The day when indigenous Australians come to regard themselves as people with a distinct historical and cultural heritage but not of a distinct race will be a day of "psychological liberation." Until then, "psychic trouble" will continue to beset Aboriginal people. "The virulent but sometimes subtle antipathy of some Australians to our existential claims is the source of the indigenous Australian anxiety," Noel claims. I'm not sure about the aetiology here, but the end aimed at is impeccable. Race is dead.

The past seems now to be Noel's latest major agenda item for the future. Resolution of the past, of memory, nostalgia and regret, is a necessity of restoration for a troubled spirit. As we age beyond mid-life, our futures have become largely our pasts. Eventually we know we have far more time behind us than ahead of us. The economy of time imposes itself. Traditions and the pasts of others gain in realism and seem less exotic. Like the dead, we who are getting older belong to history as well as to the now. The idea of the classical world as a rich Ur-state appeals perhaps more and more, as a new, if retrospective, start. My own current immersion in the world of the 1930s has this kind of appeal. There is affective security in its fixity.

There is much in Noel's essay about the importance of the Aboriginal classical cultures of the past, both for the descendants of those creative Old People but also for Australians and the world generally. He refers to the ancient myth-based song-lines of Australia, and the wide and rich linguistic and narrative heritage of the continent and its islands. There is no hyperbole in his description of these bodies of lore as the *Iliad* and *Odyssey* of Australia – they are, and they are played out on a vaster stage than the coastal Mediterranean, and in several hundred more tongues.

Noel's Cape York Partnership, of which he is chairman, has recently begun to expand its role beyond being a policy think-tank to seeking to set up a centre for Cape York Peninsula languages. Most of these scores of languages are lost or moribund or, as some say, "sleeping." Wik-Mungkan alone remains the first language of children, at Aurukun. Other remote and not so remote regions of Australia have had language centres for years or decades. They are places where recording, analysing, teaching, revitalisation and archiving of local languages and oral history take place, and written and audiovisual language aids are produced. I recall raising the Cape's gap in this domain with Noel in about 1991, but there have been other, urgent purposes with which to deal. A few years after this we also had a long phone call during which I raised with him the suggestion that "race" needed to be removed from Australian identity politics. The years have rushed by and we are, perhaps, almost there.

A very substantial archive of past language, song, ceremony, technology, art, mythology, ethno-biology, political geography and other cultural riches exists for Cape York Peninsula. Touchingly, for me anyway, Noel refers in his essay to the records of past researchers of these matters as "part of the world's heritage." The age of primary bush fieldwork of this kind in the region may not be over, but the older practitioners are getting on a bit and the emphasis is shifting to IT rather than mixing salvage ethnography with shooting pigs and digging for water.

Such wells of information make it possible for the Australian landscape very widely to have restored to it the tens of thousands of place names that were in place before the first colonial explorers and surveyors arrived. These place names have been mapped in on-the-ground detail most intensively since the heroic arrival of the four-wheel drive vehicle, from 1946, first the Canadian Blitz, then the English Land Rover, then the Japanese Toyota. Noel regards this restoration of the original toponyms as "a vitally important agenda for the country." I agree. Most of this knowledge is still dormant in the records of scholars and in the vaults of the collecting institutions. Digitisation via geographic information systems is the greatest gift to unleashing access to this treasure while allowing its long-term preservation and conservation.

What has all this to do with amending the constitution? Along with what Noel regards as the necessity for indigenous people to have a "bi-cultural future" and "psychological liberation," in his essay he deems the need for this fabulous knowledge of the past to become liberated from obscurity a necessity for the national social fabric. It is a part of the array of unfinished business between Australian peoples and their country. There will be no "more complete commonwealth" unless all Australians have added a layer of identity that connects them to such heritage: "This is the true meaning of commonwealth."

Noel's essay is not so much an offering to a debate as an announcement, albeit one full of serious care, one steeped in Australian political life, and one that draws in the magical strings of his omnivorous reading. It is a manifesto but at the same time an act of compassion, and of courage. It is not self-protective, although some readers will be left wondering who Noel's British ancestors were, having heard here about his Aboriginal grandfather, Ngulunhdhul, and great-grandfather, Arrimi, and his ill-tempered mother's mother.

For all its generosity, Noel's essay is nevertheless remorselessly tough on the left and in particular on what he identifies as their silence on the "social crisis" in many of the communities. But it comes from a big, if irascible, heart. In Australian political life it is hard to think of anyone less cynically disposed, or more passionately caring about his own and others' variously layered country-selves and identities, from the local to the national.

Peter Sutton

Paul Kelly

Noel Pearson with eloquence and insight has told the nation it cannot postpone the question still unanswered after two centuries: what is the place for the first peoples of Australia in the constitutional nation created from their ancestral lands? That is, by definition, a political and constitutional issue. It is also, however, something greater: a spiritual and conscience issue for the entire nation.

For the Australian people – conservative, liberal, socialist, Green, Anglo-Irish or ethnic – there is no escape from our shared historical dilemma. Pearson's purpose in his essay is to confront Australians with the question but also to lead them towards an answer. Time is running short. Tony Abbott is pledged to a constitutional referendum yet the precise question is undefined and the public debate remains confused and fragmentary, hardly good omens.

It is now widely accepted that reconciliation must be both practical and symbolic. Pearson has long operated as a prophet on both fronts. Indeed, his campaign to transform the debate about welfare, education and living standards in remote indigenous communities has had a profound impact on public policy. But he warns in this essay the indigenous predicament cannot be reduced to the vital yet banal "closing the gap" paradigm. Invoking the words of Galarrwuy Yunupingu, he says something greater is at stake: whether the Yolngu of Arnhem Land – along with other indigenous peoples from across the continent – will find a settled place in the Australian nation so they may long live on the earth.

It is my belief that Pearson has devised a cultural and political framing of the nation that offers the best avenue to addressing the Australian dilemma. He has been developing this framework over decades. "Our nation is in three parts," he writes. There is the ancient heritage with its culture in the land- and seascapes. There is the British heritage with its structure of law, society and governance. And there is the multicultural achievement – the merging of peoples from around the world.

Pearson argues the people of Australia now "stand on the cusp of bringing these three parts of our national story together." He suggests this is the ultimate meaning of constitutional recognition of Australia's indigenous peoples and this will make "a more complete commonwealth."

This should become Abbott's script. He could find no better method of interpreting the referendum to the Australian people. The key to this idea lies in "completing" the nation (a conservative concept) by inclusion (a liberal concept) authorised by constitutional amendment (the essence of reformism).

The prime minister likes the idea of completing the nation's constitution as opposed to transforming the constitution. It is a pivotal point: the public will vote for the former but reject the latter. This interpretation is perfect for Abbott as a constitutional conservative and monarchist. It makes possible the referendum's passage because it enables the public to grasp what it means and endorse its purpose. The idea reassures because it fulfils.

In this sense Pearson's essay hands Abbott an immense gift. Yet Abbott's door is already open. He told parliament last year that pre-1788 "this land was as Aboriginal then as it is Australian now" and that until this is acknowledged "we will be an incomplete nation and a torn people." Pearson and Abbott see the referendum not just as atoning for the past but also as fulfilling the Australian story for the future. This is the key to either persuading or marginalising conservative pundits, such as Andrew Bolt, who currently oppose the referendum and have the sway to inflict grievous harm. Unfortunately, they do not see that failing to resolve this question constitutes a far deeper threat to Australia's stability.

The essay reveals Pearson, again, as too iconoclastic to be typecast by political allegiance and too independent to be a populist among his own people. On the components of the referendum question Pearson has re-assessed. His journey testifies to the agony amid the opportunity this referendum constitutes for Aboriginal leaders. It is the eternal tribulation of politics: the trade-off between ambition and realism.

Pearson has abandoned his previous support for the referendum as a constitutional guarantee of racial non-discrimination. He makes this clear in the essay. It is an essential step, since the Abbott government would never include this provision in a referendum. Although recommended by the 2012 expert committee, the idea would derail the recognition of the indigenous peoples by creating a new and divisive debate about a constitutional bill of rights. Pearson, as realist, says constitutional change cannot be obtained by winning 51 per cent of the people. The only road to success is bringing "the whole country on board." Hence, he makes this concession; as a realist, he had no choice.

But, ambitious as ever, Pearson wants a trade-off for his concession. He asks: if a racial non-discrimination clause is not the answer, then what is a better solution? Anxious to secure more substance for the referendum, he is unconvincing in his answer. As an alternative, Pearson wants a new political body "to ensure that indigenous peoples have a voice in their own affairs." The idea is not sufficiently developed. The problem, surely, is that it seems too much a variation on dubious past experiments involving indigenous advisory or representative bodies.

However, Pearson's most powerful idea about the referendum's components goes to the question of race. In many ways this is his single most important argument in the essay. Pearson fully supports removal of the racial references in the constitution, usually seen as sections 25 and 51(xxvi). This is often called repealing the "race power."

But what happens after this? There is a strong push for a new power to be inserted permitting the Commonwealth to legislate in relation to Aboriginal and Torres Strait Islander peoples. Yet this raises another point: is the referendum supposed to eliminate the idea of race from the constitution or entrench a new race power allowing laws to be made on a racial basis for indigenous peoples alone? The answer to this question may determine whether the referendum succeeds or fails.

Here is where Pearson takes his stand. "We are a human race," he writes. He sees differences of culture, heritage, language and religion resolved in the idea of a shared race. This leads to a powerful political conclusion. The best approach for the indigenous peoples, Pearson argues, is to honour their own culture but not seek citizenship of the nation on the basis of race, nor have their racial identification embedded in the constitution. He says accepting this idea will be "a day of psychological liberation" and that removing the concept of race will have immense practical gains for indigenous peoples. Many progressives will find this idea shocking. Yet it provides the deeper basis for reconciliation.

The ultimate inspiration in this essay, however, is its fusion of the moral and practical. For Pearson, there is a moral obligation upon the Australian people to end the lack of constitutional recognition of the indigenous peoples. Beyond this lies the fate of our national project: how does Australia endure as a united cohesive nation without recognition of the peoples whose history on this continent stretches back beyond the mists of antiquity? The qualities now needed are clarity, goodwill, flexibility and realism. Noel Pearson offers them in abundance.

Paul Kelly

Robert Manne

There is one dimension of Tony Abbott's political character that does not fit with his wall-to-wall conservatism: his interest in the wellbeing, according to his lights, of Aboriginal Australia and his personal "crusade" for indigenous constitutional recognition. This dimension of Abbott's politics first became apparent in February 2013 when, as the leader of the opposition, he spoke on the *Aboriginal and Torres Strait Islander Peoples Recognition Bill*. According to Abbott, Australia was a "blessed country," except for one thing: "We have never fully made peace with the first Australians." Abbott described this failure as a "stain on our soul." Australia had to do now what should have been done 200 or 100 years ago: "acknowledge Aboriginal people in our foundation document." When he became prime minister, Abbott showed that these words were not an aberration. He began to prepare the ground carefully for a referendum on indigenous constitutional recognition and let it be known that its success was one of his most heartfelt prime-ministerial ambitions. Clearly there is something peculiar in the Abbott discrepancy – the arch-conservative genuinely interested in indigenous constitutional recognition – that needs to be explained.

My explanation begins with two words: Noel Pearson. In 2005 Pearson delivered the Mabo Oration on the place of indigenous Australians in the nation. His speech concluded with these words: "The political truism that only Nixon could go to China is pertinent here. Only a highly conservative leader, one who enjoys the confidence of the most conservative sections of the national community, will be able to lead the country to an appropriate resolution of these issues. It will take a prime minister in the mould of Tony Abbott to lead the Australian nation to settle the 'unfinished business' between settler Australians and the other people who are members of this nation: the indigenous people." This was remarkably prescient. It was also part of what Pearson describes as his political "long game." At the time Abbott was no more than a middle-ranking member of the Howard cabinet.

Under Gillard, Pearson joined the expert panel considering the question of indigenous constitutional recognition, established in the compact with the Greens. For him, however, the planets only began aligning favourably, as he put it, as it became obvious that Abbott would become the next prime minister. For Abbott, as he admitted recently, conversion to the cause of indigenous constitutional recognition was long in coming. There is every reason to believe that it came primarily because of Pearson's friendship and tuition.

Over the years it was Pearson who has made a case for constitutional recognition that might have some prospect of success. Its gradual development can be seen in the anthology of his writings, Up from the Mission. It has now been brought together in A Rightful Place. In essence the argument goes like this. Australia is a "triune nation," formed of three parts: indigenous heritage; British cultural, political and legal foundation; successful immigrant integration through the philosophy of multiculturalism. Pearson rejects the conservative anxiety that the retention of either indigenous or immigrant identity threatens to splinter the nation. In contemporary societies individuals have what he calls layered identities. Part of the identity of indigenous Australians is traditional culture, language and love of homeland; another part the education that will allow them to operate effectively in the modern economy. There is no need to choose between economic participation and fidelity to tradition.

There was once, according to Pearson, a time when indigenous Australians had no place in the nation. This time has passed – through the franchise, legal protection from racial discrimination and limited common-law access to their lands through native title. Yet full acceptance still awaits recognition in the constitution. Until that recognition, Australia will remain an incomplete nation.

As Pearson understands, constitutional change in Australia is dauntingly difficult. In left–right politics, 51 per cent support is sufficient; in constitutional politics, support must approach 90 per cent, as it did in the 1967 indigenous referendum. A long time ago, when thinking about political support for his plans to tackle the breakdown in remote Aboriginal communities, Pearson became convinced that friends of the indigenous peoples could be found among the conservatives of rural and regional Australia. In thinking now about indigenous constitutional recognition this idea, about a broad coalition including conservatives, has been extended. To garner the level of support required, the only possibility is an Australian version of the Nixon in China phenomenon. The leadership of a trusted diehard conservative like Tony Abbott is vital.

What are the prospects of success? In A Rightful Place Pearson quotes a comment made in 1959 by the anthropologist W.E.H. Stanner: "To the older generations of Australians it seemed an impossible idea that there could be anything in the Aborigines or in their tradition to admire. The contempt has perhaps almost gone." Unhappily, Stanner was wrong. In recent years, the old contempt has returned. One source is the editor of *Quadrant*, Keith Windschuttle. His revisionist history of the genocide in Tasmania not only minimises the number of deaths but also argues that Aborigines had no attachment to country and were "the agents of their own demise," that is to say responsible for their own extermination. Another source is the former Labor minister Gary Johns. Here is a typical passage from his *Aboriginal Self-Determination*. "What if the [Aboriginal] culture is no more than people behaving badly, a result of blighted environments, poor incentives, awful history, and an historic culture best relegated to museums and occasional ceremonies? ... Aborigines did not prosper in Australia. They merely survived." A third source is the News Corp columnist Andrew Bolt, who regularly attributes the contemporary malaise of life in the remote communities almost entirely to traditional Aboriginal culture and treats with sarcasm any warm-hearted description of the world of the Aborigines before the arrival of the British, while apparently blind to the racism involved.

As Pearson understands, writers like these are influential on the right of the federal parliamentary Coalition. Come the referendum it is hard to estimate how many will side with Andrew Bolt rather than Tony Abbott. Even more troublingly, such writers have created a public opinion of uncertain size contemptuous of Aborigines and hostile therefore to constitutional indigenous recognition. Pearson's political logic is based on the idea that the hard right can be isolated from Abbott-led conservatives and everyone to their left. But if the hard right cannot be contained to a rump, and if right of centre opinion is, on balance, opposed to recognition, then the referendum will most likely fail.

There is a different kind of problem with relying on an arch-conservative to lead the campaign. The Gillard-appointed expert panel favoured the removal of the idea of "race" from the constitution but also constitutional protection against racism, recognition of Aboriginal languages, and a generous declaration acknowledging and respecting the Aborigines as Australia's first peoples. As soon as their report was tabled, Tony Abbott opposed the idea of constitutional protection from racism as a mini bill of rights, a classic expression of contemporary Australian conservatism. Eventually conservative opposition to any mention of Aboriginal languages in the constitution also became clear. Even then the whittling down of the expert panel's recommendations seemed not yet complete.

A referendum on doing little more than removing references to race in the constitution would be a far from satisfactory outcome. Pearson has tried to overcome the problem of diminishing hopes by floating the idea of a stirring declaration outside the constitution, and the creation inside the constitution of an indigenous body restricted, however, to providing the parliament with advice. Whether such ideas will be supported by other indigenous leaders or by conservatives is presently unclear. I believe Pearson is right to think that the referendum is only likely to succeed if the campaign is led by a trusted conservative. Paradoxically, however, leadership of this kind might in the end reduce the scope of recognition so radically that the question put to referendum might actually be opposed by a sizeable number of indigenous Australians. Such an outcome would be, of course, grotesque.

There is another problem with this whole question. More than anyone, Noel Pearson was responsible for turning Australians' attention from exclusive interest in symbolic reconciliation to the crisis of life in the remote indigenous communities. This was an act of high political intelligence and courage. But it was not without risk. As Pearson understood, concentration on community dysfunction might revive the oldest stereotypes about Aboriginal Australians lying just beneath the surface of national consciousness. In the past years the old stereotypes have indeed resurfaced, encouraged by both the hard right's advocacy of assimilation and their expression of unconcealed contempt for indigenous culture.

Around the time Pearson broke the public silence concerning the problems of alcohol, drugs and welfare dependency, I argued that his increasingly open expression of irritation with the left, while understandable, was a political mistake. The pro-reconciliation enthusiasm of a significant section of the educated and affluent middle class was an asset that ought neither to be spurned nor taken for granted. I still think there is something to this criticism. Under the influence of Noel Pearson, John Howard first floated the idea of indigenous constitutional recognition immediately before the 2007 election. The idea was revived by the Greens in their 2010 compact with the Gillard government. As we have seen, it was strongly supported by Tony Abbott as leader of the opposition in 2013. And yet, despite the support for the referendum across the entire political spectrum, time and again it has been postponed, most recently until 2017 and the fiftieth anniversary of the 1967 referendum. The reason is dismayingly simple. The issue has never captured the national imagination.

This points to something deep. During the 1990s, under Paul Keating and Patrick Dodson, there existed an atmosphere of intense hopefulness about the role reconciliation might play in the creation of a better nation. In May 2000, at its climax, hundreds of thousands of Australians walked across the bridges of Australia in support of a reconciliation ceremony at the centenary of federation, an idea which, unforgivably, the Howard government quickly killed. The mood of hope was still not altogether extinguished, as the passions stirred by Kevin Rudd's February 2008 apology to the stolen generations demonstrated. However, in recent years that atmosphere has faded. Somehow, if the referendum is to succeed it will now have to rediscovered. Pearson is probably right to believe that unless the movement for indigenous constitutional recognition is led by a rock-solid conservative it is unlikely to succeed. The problem is that a rock-solid conservative is the least likely kind of political leader capable of reigniting the social-justice passions of Australians. If the referendum fails, it might not be as a consequence of the Great Australian Silence over the meaning of the dispossession but of something even older, the Great Australian Indifference to the fate of the Australian first peoples.

Noel Pearson is pre-eminently a political thinker concerned with outcomes. But he is also an intellectual concerned with the search for truth. Never has the tension between these two dimensions of his personality been clearer than it is in *A Rightful Place*. As a political strategist, Pearson understands that nothing is more likely to destroy the prospects of a successful referendum than a return to the fiercely partisan cultural conflicts over the nature of the dispossession which Australians called the History Wars. As an indigenous intellectual, however, he has discovered that the issue simply cannot be avoided.

The familial parts of *A Rightful Place*, where Pearson struggles to shine a personal light on these matters, form, for me at least, both the most moving and intellectually compelling dimension of the essay. He is keen to introduce his children to English literature. In the preface to an old favourite, *War of the Worlds*, about a ruinous alien invasion of London, Pearson discovers to his astonishment that H.G. Wells' inspiration was the British extermination of the indigenous Tasmanians. In the work of a contemporary English scholar, he discovers to his even greater astonishment that Charles Dickens – the author of *Great Expectations*, the book he has been reading to his daughter – was a bitter enemy of savage peoples: "I am yet to work out whether, how and when to tell my girl that the creator of Pip, Pumblechook and that convict wretch Magwitch may have wished her namesake great-great grandmother off the face of the earth." Pearson knows that missionaries saved his people. But he concludes this chapter with the chilling story told by one of these missionaries of the murder of Didegal, a contemporary of his great-grandfather. "Anonymous, extrajudicial, unreported, mundane. Like eradicating vermin. Or inferior beings of human likeness."

All this points to the most obvious contradiction at the heart of *A Rightful Place*. Pearson believes that the successful passage of the referendum for indigenous constitutional recognition relies on conservative leadership. For someone who is seeking to rally conservatives to the cause of constitutional recognition nothing could be more impolitic than to dwell upon the meaning of the dispossession or even to embrace, as he does, the concept of genocide as a descriptor for the nineteenth-century disaster in Tasmania and maybe elsewhere. Even some left-wing historians now avoid it. Pearson understands only too well the tension between his political pragmatism and his obligation to analyse the history of his people truthfully. "I hoped to avoid the past, but it is not possible. I hoped to dis-remember the past, but it is not possible." Pearson is too honest either to avert his gaze from history or to pretend that he has found a way to resolve the consequent contradiction.

Robert Manne

This is a revised and expanded version of a piece that appeared in the *Saturday Paper* on 27 September 2014.

Fred Chaney

A Rightful Place is another powerful contribution by Noel Pearson to public issues we prefer to avoid. While he provides a balanced description of the contesting forces around the telling of our history, his preparedness to face the brutal reality of the destruction of the Tasmanian people is welcome.

Noel is much respected by conservative Australians and they in particular should be exposed to all his views and not just to the many they find comforting, such as demands for responsibility and welfare reform. The dispossession, dispersal and, often, destruction of indigenous populations across Australia are as much part of our history as the fortitude of settlers in confronting harsh and difficult conditions, the building of a modern democracy, and the bravery of our soldiers in successive wars. We are entitled to be proud of our successes and achievements as a nation, but should avoid masking the darker aspects of our past.

Equally confronting to conservatives is the prospect of continuing Aboriginal collectives going neither peacefully into history nor foregoing their desire to retain distinct cultural identities as one layer of Australia's ongoing identity.

And yes, constitutional recognition is important and relevant to our future as a nation. It is easy for us to agree that it would be good to remove race from the constitution. It is easy to agree we need a continuing constitutional power to legislate to deal with matters such as native title, now established in our law as something peculiarly available to those who are part of the tribes or polities of First Peoples, First Nations, call them what you will, and whose collective identity as native title holders is defined through their own laws and customs. What is less easy to determine is how to give substance to constitutional recognition. Around what proposition can the nation coalesce as we managed to do in 1967?

Pearson's essay does not purport to answer this question fully. It is part of the continuing debate and argument about what form of recognition should be put before the Australian people. Eventually that will be determined by parliament, with the assistance of the parliamentary committee led by Ken Wyatt and Nova Peris and the review panel led by John Anderson. Noel's essay contributes to that debate. But the aspect of the essay which most interests me is how we deal with the long-term place of indigenous peoples within the Australian nation, how we deal with what he describes as the "existential anxieties of distinct peoples" about their survival and having a "proper and rightful place" in the nation.

The essay recognises that reconciliation is about more than the gap in economic and social circumstances. That gap is, of course, important and is widely acknowledged. What is also important, but more difficult to comprehend, is that reconciliation is also about survival of indigenous collectives as distinct peoples, with a continuing place within the Australian nation.

There is much goodwill at government and community levels about closing the social and economic gaps. In part, that is because it is in accord with our natural tendency to see assimilation as the answer. Some, such as Gary Johns, are overt in putting a negative view about indigenous culture, the virulence of which "indicates a depth of antipathy that is rooted in a troubled history." Whatever the source, *A Rightful Place*, correctly in my view, asserts that the default position (what I would call the visceral response) of many of us remains assimilationist. So we find it easy to embrace Closing the Gap, making "them" all the same as "us." That was the spirit of the 1967 referendum, as I remember it. It was a demand for equal citizenship.

This time, we are grappling with issues relating to continuing separate identities. This is more difficult for us. Noel tries to explain it and make it acceptable to us through the concept of layered identities. He gives the example of the Jewish community participating fully and at a high level in every aspect of the life of the nation while holding strongly to its own identity and practice.

It is helpful to read this essay alongside a viewing of Noel's address at Garma this year, published on YouTube. There you get the force of presentation as well as intellect. Following reference to the destruction of Tasmanian Aboriginal people, he posed the question "we are still grappling with today": "will European settlement of Australia enable a different people with a different heritage to have space in it?" He poses it as a question still unresolved. He says that in the 1820s in Tasmania we answered the question by our actions. Then in stark terms he suggests, "If we don't come to a just answer to that question today, that same answer will come about for benign reasons." If he is correct in this, and I think he is, it is a matter of great seriousness for all of us.

There is much in Australia today to suggest that we are not very interested in allowing room for indigenous cultures to continue to be part of our national fabric. Whatever lip service we offer the world's oldest living cultures, the clear message from our actions is that our main concern is to bring indigenous individuals into full enjoyment of their rights and duties as Australian citizens. There is no clear message that we understand and value these cultures as part of our nation. There is no indication from our actions that we will preserve sufficient space for the Yolngu, the Nyiyaparli, the Nyungar and so on to retain collective identities and distinctive cultural spaces.

In the case of remote communities that still observe practices close to those of pre-settlement cultures, the policies of successive governments seem designed to strangle them.

This issue poses challenges to both the broader community and the Aboriginal and Torres Strait Islander communities.

The challenge to the broader community is initially one of comprehension. If we achieve that comprehension, the next challenge is to set policies that allow difference. We won't be able to meet that challenge unless indigenous voices can be heard and have a genuine say in decisions which affect them. The essay begins to address this and has already sparked further conversations about how this might be done.

It is for the indigenous population to decide how serious they are about preserving their collective identities and how they wish to speak with authority for those identities. In *Radical Hope*, Quarterly Essay 35 (2009), Noel captured, in a single sentence about a great Crow leader, Plenty Coups, the challenging task facing today's indigenous leaders: he "led his people through the door to an unknowable future, and he stood his people on their feet to contend with the new world."

Through native title, the raw material for legally acknowledging collective identities exists. Around Australia, claims both determined and undetermined document collective identities and their memberships. Even where native title is deemed to be extinguished, the process can identify who speaks for country, who the tribe is, and what the territory is. The Yorta Yorta spokeswoman Monica Morgan reacted to the dismissal of their appeal against the denial of their native title by saying firmly, we are Yorta Yorta, we are here, and you have to deal with us. In the same way the substantially dispossessed Nyungars, with the reality of massive extinguishment of native title across their territories, have been able to be at the table with the State as the traditional owners of the southwest of Western Australia.

In this respect, the assertion on page 67, that "there is no official recognition of the many tribal nations associated with particular territories," is incorrect and is contradicted by Noel himself on page 69: "Through land rights schemes [and] native title rights … much has been done to recognise the territorial rights of … the original Aboriginal and Torres Strait Islander tribes." If indigenous people are serious in wanting to address the power imbalance caused by their extreme minority status, native title alone is an opportunity to have a place at the table as negotiators rather than supplicants.

The essay has already sparked discussion about how the democratic imbalance Noel identifies might be rectified. A few designated seats in parliament would be unlikely to produce members with authority to speak for the whole indigenous community. To what body would legislative proposals affecting indigenous people and peoples be referred? Who does speak for indigenous Australia? Or does each of the hundreds of indigenous cultural groups speak for itself? These are questions which only indigenous people themselves can answer.

It should not be so hard to progress discussion on these issues. Post-*Mabo* it is part of Australia's reality that First Peoples, identified through traditional law and custom as a native title group, have particular rights peculiar to them over identified territories. Numerous mining and other agreements are made with indigenous people not as individuals but as members of traditionally based collectives. Those involved are fully Australian citizens and are also fully members of Aboriginal polities, with a group as well as an individual identity. What Pearson's essay describes are the existential anxieties of these distinct peoples about whether they can survive and have a "proper and rightful place" in the nation. They will only do so if, to borrow again from Quarterly Essay 35, they are a serious people able to speak for themselves: "Do we have the seriousness necessary to maintain our languages, traditions and knowledge?"

I hope that *A Rightful Place* will promote the discussions required in general and indigenous communities about the challenges they both face. As a member of the general community, I hope governments and communities will ensure that there is space and time to permit indigenous people to work through these issues and for us to get beyond our instinctive demand for assimilation.

Fred Chaney

Fred Chaney was minister for Aboriginal Affairs in the Fraser government and has been involved in indigenous affairs since the 1960s in a variety of roles, including in the areas of reconciliation and native title. He was named Senior Australian of the Year in 2014.

Megan Davis is professor of law at the University of New South Wales, where she is director of the Indigenous Law Centre. She was a member of the Expert Panel on Constitutional Recognition of Aboriginal and Torres Strait Islander Peoples.

John Hirst was a member of the history department at La Trobe University from 1968 to 2007. His books include *Australian History in 7 Questions, Freedom on the Fatal Shore, Sense & Nonsense in Australian History* and *The Shortest History of Europe.*

Paul Kelly is editor-at-large of the *Australian.* His books about Australian politics include *The End of Certainty, The March of Patriots* and *Triumph and Demise.*

Celeste Liddle is an Arrernte woman living in Melbourne, and the National Aboriginal and Torres Strait Islander organiser for the National Tertiary Education Union. She has written for the *Guardian*, Fairfax and *Tracker*, among others.

Robert Manne is emeritus professor of politics at La Trobe University. His recent books include *Making Trouble: Essays Against the New Complacency* and *The Words that Made Australia* (as co-editor). A festschrift was published in 2013: *State of the Nation: Essays for Robert Manne.*

Rachel Perkins is a director, producer and screenwriter. In 1992 she founded Blackfella Films. Her work includes the films *Radiance, One Night the Moon* and *Mabo*, as well as the documentary series *First Australians.* Perkins is an Arrernte woman from Central Australia, who was raised in Canberra.

Henry Reynolds' ground-breaking histories include *The Other Side of the Frontier, Dispossession, The Law of the Land, Why Weren't We Told?* and *Forgotten War.* In 2000 he took up a professorial fellowship at the University of Tasmania.

Guy Rundle is Crikey's correspondent-at-large. A frequent contributor to a range of publications in Australia and the UK, he was editor of *Arena Magazine* for fifteen years. He has written several hit stage shows for Max Gillies and is the author of, among others, Quarterly Essay 3, *The Opportunist, Down to the Crossroads*, an account of the 2008 US presidential election, and *A Revolution in the Making: Robots, 3D Printing and the Future.*

Peter Sutton is an author, anthropologist and linguist, who has been a student of Aboriginal Australia, especially Cape York Peninsula, for several decades. His most recent book is *The Politics of Suffering*. He works at the South Australian Museum and the University of Adelaide.

SUBSCRIBE to Quarterly Essay & SAVE over 25% on the cover price

Subscriptions: Receive a discount and never miss an issue. Mailed direct to your door.

☐ **1 year subscription** (4 issues): $59 within Australia incl. GST. Outside Australia $89.

☐ **2 year subscription** (8 issues): $105 within Australia incl. GST. Outside Australia $165.

* All prices include postage and handling.

Back Issues: (Prices include postage and handling.)

☐ **QE 2** ($15.99) John Birmingham *Appeasing Jakarta*
☐ **QE 4** ($15.99) Don Watson *Rabbit Syndrome*
☐ **QE 6** ($15.99) John Button *Beyond Belief*
☐ **QE 7** ($15.99) John Martinkus *Paradise Betrayed*
☐ **QE 8** ($15.99) Amanda Lohrey *Groundswell*
☐ **QE 10** ($15.99) Gideon Haigh *Bad Company*
☐ **QE 11** ($15.99) Germaine Greer *Whitefella Jump Up*
☐ **QE 12** ($15.99) David Malouf *Made in England*
☐ **QE 13** ($15.99) Robert Manne with David Corlett *Sending Them Home*
☐ **QE 14** ($15.99) Paul McGeough *Mission Impossible*
☐ **QE 15** ($15.99) Margaret Simons *Latham's World*
☐ **QE 17** ($15.99) John Hirst *"Kangaroo Court"*
☐ **QE 18** ($15.99) Gail Bell *The Worried Well*
☐ **QE 19** ($15.99) Judith Brett *Relaxed & Comfortable*
☐ **QE 20** ($15.99) John Birmingham *A Time for War*
☐ **QE 21** ($15.99) Clive Hamilton *What's Left?*
☐ **QE 22** ($15.99) Amanda Lohrey *Voting for Jesus*
☐ **QE 23** ($15.99) Inga Clendinnen *The History Question*
☐ **QE 24** ($15.99) Robyn Davidson *No Fixed Address*
☐ **QE 25** ($15.99) Peter Hartcher *Bipolar Nation*
☐ **QE 26** ($15.99) David Marr *His Master's Voice*
☐ **QE 27** ($15.99) Ian Lowe *Reaction Time*
☐ **QE 28** ($15.99) Judith Brett *Exit Right*

☐ **QE 29** ($15.99) Anne Manne *Love & Money*
☐ **QE 30** ($15.99) Paul Toohey *Last Drinks*
☐ **QE 31** ($15.99) Tim Flannery *Now or Never*
☐ **QE 32** ($15.99) Kate Jennings *American Revolution*
☐ **QE 33** ($15.99) Guy Pearse *Quarry Vision*
☐ **QE 34** ($15.99) Annabel Crabb *Stop at Nothing*
☐ **QE 36** ($15.99) Mungo MacCallum *Australian Story*
☐ **QE 37** ($15.99) Waleed Aly *What's Right?*
☐ **QE 38** ($15.99) David Marr *Power Trip*
☐ **QE 39** ($15.99) Hugh White *Power Shift*
☐ **QE 42** ($15.99) Judith Brett *Fair Share*
☐ **QE 43** ($15.99) Robert Manne *Bad News*
☐ **QE 44** ($15.99) Andrew Charlton *Man-Made World*
☐ **QE 45** ($15.99) Anna Krien *Us and Them*
☐ **QE 46** ($15.99) Laura Tingle *Great Expectations*
☐ **QE 47** ($15.99) David Marr *Political Animal*
☐ **QE 48** ($15.99) Tim Flannery *After the Future*
☐ **QE 49** ($15.99) Mark Latham *Not Dead Yet*
☐ **QE 50** ($15.99) Anna Goldsworthy *Unfinished Business*
☐ **QE 51** ($15.99) David Marr *The Prince*
☐ **QE 52** ($15.99) Linda Jaivin *Found in Translation*
☐ **QE 53** ($15.99) Paul Toohey *That Sinking Feeling*
☐ **QE 54** ($15.99) Andrew Charlton *Dragon's Tail*
☐ **QE 55** ($15.99) Noel Pearson *A Rightful Place*

Payment Details: I enclose a cheque/money order made out to Schwartz Publishing Pty Ltd. Please debit my credit card (Mastercard or Visa accepted).

Card No. ☐☐☐☐ ☐☐☐☐ ☐☐☐☐ ☐☐☐☐

Expiry date / **CCV** **Amount $**

Cardholder's name **Signature**

Name

Address

Email **Phone**

Post or fax this form to: Quarterly Essay, Reply Paid 79448, Collingwood VIC 3066 / Tel: (03) 9486 0288 / Fax: (03) 9486 0244 / Email: subscribe@blackincbooks.com
Subscribe online at **www.quarterlyessay.com**

www.ingramcontent.com/pod-product-compliance
Lightning Source LLC
Chambersburg PA
CBHW081402270326
41930CB00015B/3382